She Dreams

Study Guide with Leader Helps

Live the Life You Were Created For

She DREAMS

Tiffany Bluhm

Study Guide with Leader Helps

Nashville | Abingdon Women

She Dreams
Live the Life You Were Created For
Study Guide with Leader Helps

Copyright © 2019 Abingdon Press
All rights reserved.

No part of this work may be reproduced or transmitted in any form or by any means, electronic or mechanical, including photocopying and recording, or by any information storage or retrieval system, except as may be expressly permitted by the 1976 Copyright Act or in writing from the publisher. Requests for permission can be addressed to Permissions, The United Methodist Publishing House, 2222 Rosa L. Parks Blvd., Nashville, TN 37228-1306 or e-mailed to permissions@umpublishing.org.

ISBN 978-1-5018-7834-3

Unless otherwise indicated, all Scripture quotations are taken from the Holy Bible, New Living Translation, copyright ©1996, 2004, 2015 by Tyndale House Foundation. Used by permission of Tyndale House Publishers, Inc., Carol Stream, Illinois 60188. All rights reserved.

Scripture noted NKJV is taken from the New King James Version®. Copyright © 1982 by Thomas Nelson. Used by permission. All rights reserved.

19 20 21 22 23 24 25 26 27 28 — 10 9 8 7 6 5 4 3 2 1
MANUFACTURED IN THE UNITED STATES OF AMERICA

Contents

About the Author 6

Introduction 7

She Dreams Declaration 11

Week 1: You Were Born for This
The Birth of Moses (Exodus 1:1–2:15) 12
Group Session Guide 31

Week 2: God-Sized Dreams
Moses in Midian (Exodus 2:15–4:17) 36
Group Session Guide 52

Week 3: Fighting for the Dream
Moses in Egypt (Exodus 4:18–12:32) 56
Group Session Guide 74

Week 4: Don't Give Up on the Daydream
Moses Leads the Exodus (Exodus 12:32–15:21) 80
Group Session Guide 99

Week 5: Growing Pains
Moses in the Wilderness (Exodus 15:22–19:6) 104
Group Session Guide 119

Week 6: Be(coming) the Dreamer
Moses Inspires Others to Dream (Exodus 19:6–40) 124
Group Session Guide 142

Leader Helps 146

Notes 155

About the Author

Tiffany Bluhm is a speaker and writer who is passionate about helping women come to know their worth, value, and purpose because of a loving, redeeming God. In an engaging and relevant approach that speaks to women right where they are, she shares insights from a life spent chasing after Jesus while walking alongside women from suburbia to the inner city, jails and brothels, and the slums of Kolkata. Because of her own story of international adoption and the adoption of a son from Uganda, Tiffany has a heart for women and children in the margins and has created a number of unconventional outreaches to serve them. In addition to speaking regularly at conferences and events, she leads a local gathering called Sip and Savor, where women break bread, study God's Word, and commune with God and one another. Tiffany writes for a number of online and print publications as well as popular blogs, including The Bible App, ScaryMommy.com, and her own weekly blog at TiffanyBluhm.com. She lives in Tacoma, Washington, with her husband and two sons.

Follow Tiffany:

- @tiffanybluhm
- @tiffanybluhm
- @TiffanyABluhm

Blog   TiffanyBluhm.com (check here for event dates and booking information)

Introduction

As a child, what did you dream you would be when you grew up? Did you imagine yourself as a doctor? A teacher? An astronaut? When I was nine years old, I dreamed of being a farmer. True story. I had wild fantasies about collecting fresh eggs from my chickens, milking my spotted cows, and feeding fat, squishy pigs. I would daydream about my expansive farm with all sorts of animals that would feed my family. At that age I failed to take into account the manual labor needed to run the farm of my dreams. So as I grew, my dream of farm life was replaced with a more...well...sedentary dream.

Next I dreamed of being a playwright. I wanted to write stories that others would act out on the world's stage for all to admire. Theatergoers would leave their seats inspired by the heroic acts of my characters. Then as a young adult I dreamed of being a lawyer because I liked the idea of pantsuits, a briefcase, and arguing my point for a purpose. All of these dreams of what I would someday *be* were actually more about what I would *do*, and they didn't necessarily take into account the woman I was *becoming*.

Only as my God-given gifts emerged did I see the thread that pulled all those past dreams together. I realized that rather than being a farmer, playwright, or lawyer, what I really dreamed of was shepherding, leading, operating out of conviction and compassion, and telling stories that mattered—ones that would bring hope and grace to an otherwise dark world. *These* are the dreams that were given to me by the Father. All of who I am—my experiences, gifts, passions, setbacks, and insecurities—is subject to Him; and He is calling me, inviting me, to dream glorious, majestic dreams with Him for my good and His glory.

The same is true for you, friend! You were created to partner with God for the glorious dreams He has for you! Your dreams—the ones that beat in your heart and keep you up at night—matter. As you chase after the Dream Giver and live the life you were created for, everything changes. You won't be the same person; you'll become *all* that God has designed you to be! The only requirement is your willingness to use your skills, gifts, and strengths as you trust in the Dream Giver.

Through my own journey, I've discovered that our dreams of who we will become are far more important to the Father than what we will accomplish in this life. Yes, He has dreams for you and me, but first He longs for us to know Him, trust Him, and love Him; then we can partner with Him for dreams that will draw us even closer to His heart, spark joy in our spirits, and help us to become women of incredible faith and virtue.

Over the next six weeks we will explore our own dreams as we look to the story of Moses and his journey to live out the God-sized dream given to him, mining the ancient wisdom and truth God offers each of us with a dream beating in our heart. Through our study we will identify the role of prayer as we grow into our dreams, the importance of obedience as we pursue what God has for us, why our dreams are a blessing not only to us but also to others, how our failures can be a gift in the journey toward our dreams becoming reality, and what role we play as we partner with God for the impossible.

Getting Started

What You Need

For this six-week journey you will need both the *She Dreams* book (available separately) and this study guide, which includes personal lessons for each week as well as guided outlines for six group sessions (if you are meeting with a group). These outlines offer a roadmap that you can use as you either follow along or facilitate the session, if you are the leader (more on that below). Video segments for the group sessions are also available separately (DVD or streaming).

Your Personal Study

For each week of study there are five days of personal lessons, alternating between days when your focus is on studying the Scriptures and days when your focus is on reading a chapter from the book; but on every day you will be reflecting and making application to your life and your dreams. So, two lessons each week will instruct you to read a chapter in the book (they're not too long, I promise!), and three lessons each week will guide you in digging into the Scriptures. I think you'll find it to be a very manageable rhythm, but don't feel bound by it. If you want to read both chapters for the week in one sitting, go for it! Or you might even prefer to read the entire book in one or two sittings and then just review the chapters as you make your way through the lessons. If that's your jam, great! Let your schedule and the Holy Spirit lead you to the routine or plan that's best for you.

Completing the lessons each week will help to prepare you for the discussion and activities of the group session. But if life happens and you just can't finish the lessons before the group session, don't let that keep you from showing up, listening, and participating. I promise you'll get something from it—as well as bless the others in your group just by being present and contributing who you are, as only you can. (In case you're wondering, it's recommended that you do the study with a group for the tremendous benefit of shared insights, support, and encouragement; however, a self-guided study is also possible.)

Meeting with a Group

When studying with a group, you'll gather each week to watch a video, discuss what you're learning, and pray together. The session outlines, which provide options for both a 60-minute and a 90-minute session, include discussion questions, activities, prayer prompts, and notes for the video segment. You'll find the outline for each session at the end of the personal lessons for that week.

If you're the facilitator or leader of your group, you'll want to check out the additional leader helps at the back of this book. Ideally group members should complete the first week of lessons before your first group session. This is because each video message complements the content that you have studied during that week. (But the world won't stop turning if you watch the video first. I'm all about freedom!) Whether or not your group watches the video, the questions and activities will guide you in sharing your hopes, struggles, and victories as you seek to discover and pursue your God-given dreams together.

Depending on life circumstances and schedules, some groups might choose to extend the study, devoting two weeks to every session. In that case, you could choose to watch the video during the first session and devote the second session to discussion, giving group members two weeks to complete the lessons. Again, feel free to adapt the study as you wish to meet the needs of your particular group.

A Final Word

As we make this journey together, I dare you to dream the impossible dreams the Lord is stirring in your heart, reclaim broken dreams, and trust God for the victory. May you dream as you've never dreamed before, chasing dreams of restoration, resurrection, and redemption. And may the Dream Giver lift you up and draw you closer by His miraculous grace and kindness.

No matter what has happened to you in the past; no matter your skills, gifts, or doubts—the Dream Giver calls to you. He loves you and will be all that you need. Say yes to the majesty and mystery of a life with the One who loved you even before you took your first breath.

I'm praying for you. I'm praying that no excuse, doubt, or fear robs you of what the good Lord longs to do in you as you chase dreams that bring health, wholeness, and goodness to your own life and the lives of those around you.

Tiffany

She Dreams

She dreams of sunlight, strong winds, and victory.
She dreams of a majestic story, a whimsical mystery.

She dreams of life abundant, so free and wild.
She dreams of the Father's call to her, "Beloved child."

She dreams of slaying dragons, saving the day,
She dreams of taking her place at the feet of Yahweh.

She dreams in vivid colors, jewel tones, and pastels.
She dreams of freedom and truth, like the clangs of the Liberty Bell.

She dreams of teaching, leading, and serving.
She dreams of a journey of which she is deserving.

She dreams of grace, mercy, and hope.
She dreams of thriving not just learning to cope.

She dreams of rushing peace like a river.
She dreams of the one and only Dream Giver.

—Tiffany Bluhm

Week 1

You Were Born for This

The Birth of Moses
(Exodus 1:1–2:15)

You were built for great dreams
as you partner with God.

DAY 1: THE WORLD NEEDS YOU TO DREAM

When I read the story of Moses, I find myself lost in the narrative. With a story full of loss, gains, bravery, doubt, and victory, he is no different from you or me. He had a human heart that dreamed of greater things for himself, his people, and his world. You and I dream of those things, too. We dream of a life well lived—one of hope and courage, mystery and victory. We want our own story of dreams becoming reality, dreams resurrected, and dreams redeemed. The truth is, you and I were built for it. We each deserve a life we love with the Lover of our lives, the very One who will lead us each and every step of the way.

As we will see throughout his journey in the Book of Exodus, Moses grew in strength, faith, and tenacity for the ways of the Father. His heart softened to the plans of God, and the plans of God soon became the dreams of his own heart—dreams that changed the course of his life, his family, and an entire nation. Like Moses' dreams, our own God-sized dreams change us. They invite us to be the best versions of ourselves. They call us to take risks and sacrifice the good things of life for the greatest things. They draw us to deeply depend on the Dream Giver—the One who whispers to us through a burning bush, the One who parts the Red Sea, and the One who gives us the Promised Land of our hearts. He will not leave us nor forsake us.

Every woman deserves to live a life of beauty, passion, adventure, and purpose. Our dreams, no matter how big or how small, push us to become women of courage, grace, and grit. We were born to dream. In His goodness, God redeems our very lives, breathes dreams within our hearts, and revives the dreams that have died. He invites us to trust Him as we dream impossible dreams that only He can bring to pass—because God not only gives dreams; He fulfills them.

As you journey through this study about dreams and live into the life you were created for, may you relate to Moses' story as a dreamer who dreams impossible dreams that draw you closer to the Father and change your life, your world, and your future. You, my friend, are smarter, stronger, and more gifted and capable than you think you are. There is more than meets the eye. Your darkest moment and your brightest moment work together. Nothing is lost on the Dream Giver. He works every detail for your good. Even now as you read this, He is at the helm, guiding you and your days for His glory and your gain.

My fellow dreamer, allow yourself to get caught up in the mystery and majesty of the story of your own life, because there is so much the Dream Giver longs to do in you and with you. He is for you all the days of your life.

Read Chapter 1 of the *She Dreams* book, "You Were Born for This," noting below any insights or encouragement you gain from your reading:

Who are some of the dreamers in your world? What have they accomplished, and why are they inspiring to you?

DAY 2: UNFULFILLED LONGING

Have you ever thought to yourself, "How is this my life?" I sure have. On the days that kick me in the gut, I'm caught shaking my head and wondering why on earth my life is playing out like it is. "Why, God? What are you up to? Do you have a plan? I sure hope so." We wonder why our story hasn't progressed. We wonder why plans, even good plans, aren't coming to pass. We long for things to move along when they appear to be stalled. The longing can feel like too much. Whether it's longing for a loved one to know the Lord, for financial freedom, for a new job, for a spouse you can love and trust, or for the child you thought would be sleeping in your spare room by now, if left longing for too long, the heart grows weary and struggles to keep dreaming and praying for resolve.

What longing in this season of life is unfulfilled?

How has your unfulfilled longing affected your view of God?

In a perfect world, what would it look like for your longing to be fulfilled?

Each of us can be found longing for what seems completely out of reach. We wear out our knees in prayer but secretly wonder if our hopes and prayers will ever be heard and answered. Even when we don't see how it could all work out, our God is at work. He is maneuvering—guiding our days, our interactions, and our hearts for dreams that matter to the Kingdom and bring hope to the harbor of our hearts.

> Sometimes the dreams of God become our own when we least expect it. We may be discontent or living a life we love, and all the while the Lord is preparing our hearts for even greater things than we can imagine. We may not sense it, but He is setting the stage for something glorious, wondrous, and perhaps even downright terrifying.

> Moses, a hero of the Old Testament, knew a thing or two about God-size dreams. Like us, he was chosen for great and mighty plans before he was even born. The Lord placed him in Egypt on purpose for a purpose. Moses would foreshadow the coming King who would redeem us all. When he was growing up, I bet Moses had no idea of all God planned. Before we see Moses do extraordinary things in the name of justice and freedom, we see his rocky beginning, the place where all good stories start. . . .
>
> It is heartbreaking to think of a mama laying her baby in a basket and sending him down a river in hopes he'll be rescued rather than die at the hands of evil, jealous men. Yet in His power and sovereignty God not only spared Moses' life but also had a plan for his life—from before he was even born.
>
> —*She Dreams*, pages 14, 17

Read Exodus 1 in your Bible. Why were the Israelites enslaved in Egypt?

What decree preceded Moses' birth?

Before Pharaoh issued the decree to throw every Hebrew baby boy into the Nile River, we read of strong women—lying midwives who, in an act of civil disobedience to Pharaoh's order to kill baby boys upon delivery, protected the lives of innocent babies. They dreamed of life when Pharaoh dreamed of death. They feared God more than they feared Pharaoh. God was good to them. They dreamed of health, wholeness, and life for their people, and God blessed them with families of their own.

Sadly, in an act of genocide, Pharaoh gave orders to drown and thus annihilate all the Hebrew baby boys simply for being Hebrew. The Hebrew midwives had bravely defied Pharaoh with their lies, but that did not stop him from carrying out his heinous plan. Before we even witness the birth of Moses, we know his survival would be classified as a crime against the king of Egypt. He shouldn't have survived his tragic beginning, but God's way squashes the plans of even the most evil ruler.

In your opinion, what did Pharaoh fear the most, and what prompted this fear?

What role did the Hebrew midwives play, and how does this affect your understanding of God's plans?

God promoted lowly Hebrew midwives in the kingdom over an evil ruler. The midwives' duty was to protect and usher in new life. But Pharaoh demanded they violate their duty by murdering the baby boys upon birth. Pharaoh wished to kill Hebrew boys, yet we see that these Hebrew women were quite capable of bucking the system of the day because their God-sized dreams surpassed the wishes of their slave driver. The Lord used women—poor Hebrew women—to put His plans into motion. He was working even in the shadows of Exodus 1, positioning the right people in the right places to see the dreams of Israel's patriarchs—Abraham, Isaac, and Jacob—come to pass.

To understand the significance of Moses' story, it's important to know how the Israelites came to settle in Egypt generations earlier. As we've seen, the first five verses of Exodus tell us that Jacob, or Israel—father of the nation of Israel—moved to Egypt with eleven of his sons and their families to join his son Joseph. But we must look to Genesis to learn why Joseph was already there.

Joseph's brothers sold him into slavery (Genesis 37); and after he endured a difficult period involving wrongful imprisonment and interpretation of dreams, he found himself before the pharaoh of Egypt (Genesis 39–41). When Pharaoh elevated him to a prominent position, one of influence and oversight, Joseph oversaw a plan to store away grain in order to see the people through a seven-year drought. The drought resulted in a famine in Canaan as well, and so Jacob sent his sons to Egypt to buy grain. Joseph recognized his brothers and eventually reconciled with them, even after they had abandoned him (Genesis 42–45). With Joseph's invitation, Jacob and all of his family came to live in Egypt, settling in the land of Goshen (Genesis 46–47). The Israelites remained in Egypt, multiplying greatly until the time of Moses.

As a son of Jacob, a grandson of Isaac, and a great-grandson of Abraham, Joseph held within his family line a promise from God that would not be stopped.

The Promise to the Patriarchs of Israel

Abraham

[18]So the Lord made a covenant with Abram that day and said, "I have given this land to your descendants, all the way from the border of Egypt to the great Euphrates River—[19]the land now occupied by the Kenites, Kenizzites, Kadmonites, [20]Hittites, Perizzites, Rephaites, [21]Amorites, Canaanites, Girgashites, and Jebusites."

(Genesis 15:18-21)

Isaac

[2]The Lord appeared to Isaac and said, "Do not go down to Egypt, but do as I tell you. [3]Live here as a foreigner in this land, and I will be with you and bless you. I hereby confirm that I will give all these lands to you and your descendants, just as I solemnly promised Abraham, your father. [4]I will cause your descendants to become as numerous as the stars of the sky, and I will give them all these lands. And through your descendants all the nations of the earth will be blessed."

(Genesis 26:2-4)

Jacob

[13]At the top of the stairway stood the Lord, and he said, "I am the Lord, the God of your grandfather Abraham, and the God of your father, Isaac. The ground you are lying on belongs to you. I am giving it to you and your descendants. [14]Your descendants will be as numerous as the dust of the earth! They will spread out in all directions—to the west and the east, to the north and the south. And all the families of the earth will be blessed through you and your descendants. [15]What's more, I am with you, and I will protect you wherever you go. One day I will bring you back to this land. I will not leave you until I have finished giving you everything I have promised you."

(Genesis 28:13-15)

What did God promise the patriarchs of Israel?

What do you learn about the character of God from these passages?

Our God is a promise keeper. How we envision His promise might be different from what it will actually look like, but God is faithful no matter what. He did not forget His promises to His beloved people, and the people of God held on to His promise—even though they didn't necessarily see how or when it would play out. We see this evidenced at the end of Genesis 50.

Look up Genesis 50:22-26 in your Bible and record the promise of God that Joseph mentions.

Even though Joseph was rejected and abandoned by his brothers, he did not lose faith in his God. He held on to hope and the dreams that God gave him. The dreams did not come to pass in a carefree manner, but they did come to pass. In his own life, Joseph experienced periods of unfulfilled longing, and his descendants certainly did as well.

We see that before Moses ever took his first breath, heaven was orchestrating a plan of deliverance for the people of God by the hand of God. Dreams were in motion. Promises had been made, and the Lord intended to keep them. Even when we are overcome with unfulfilled longing, we can trust that the Lord is faithful and just in our lives.

Offer your unfulfilled hopes and dreams to God, asking Him to make Himself plain in your life. If you want, write your prayer below.

DAY 3: EVERY STORY HAS A BEGINNING

Read chapter 2 of the *She Dreams* book, "Broken Dreams," noting below any insights or encouragement you gain from your reading:

Think about your story of origin—where you were born, the circumstances surrounding your birth, and details about your parents or family. When you consider your beginning in this world, does it evoke happy thoughts, painful reminders, or a mixture of both? Explain your answer.

No woman on earth has the privilege of choosing how she starts out in this life. You and I don't have the option to pick if we are born into a family that is rich or poor, carefree or facing impossible challenges. We are each brought into this world innocent and unaware of the circumstances surrounding our beginning. That which we cannot control greets us in our most vulnerable state: childhood.

As grown women, our dreams are directly affected by the experiences we had in our childhood and adolescence. Try as we might, we can't gloss over the hard parts that directly affect the way we think, feel, and experience the world. If money was tight, if a parent or caregiver spoke harsh words, if there was something we couldn't control but it directly influenced how we felt about ourselves, then there's a good chance those feelings still reside within us and affect how we dream. Maybe we dream of stability because our family of origin was in a constant state of transition, or perhaps we dream of financial freedom because we felt the pangs of hunger or want when money was tight and there wasn't enough to go around. As adults, we almost always carry our childhood and adolescent experiences and understandings of the world into the life of our dreams. We will see this in Moses' life as well.

Three key women are mentioned when the Scriptures first introduce us to baby Moses: his mama, his sister, and his adoptive mother, Pharaoh's daughter. But this is no ordinary birth story! Each woman knew the decree of Pharaoh to toss all baby boys into the Nile River, and each made a choice that directly violated this order.

His mother, Jochebed, the woman who carried him for nine months and who, I imagine, tearfully placed her baby in a tar-covered basket among the reeds, was a woman of great strength and bravery. This dear woman hid her precious boy for three months but could no longer hide him, and by God's grace she witnessed the divine hand of Yahweh save her son.

After we read of Moses' mother, we read of his older sister, who followed that basket until it washed up at the feet of Pharaoh's daughter. This brave sister approached royalty, to whom she was enslaved, and explained that she could help by calling for a Hebrew woman to nurse the baby. Moses' mother appeared and was then paid to nurse her own precious baby by the request of Pharaoh's daughter.

Pharaoh's daughter assumed the baby in the basket was Hebrew and appeared to have no qualms asking a Hebrew woman to nurse the sweet little boy. Keep in mind that Pharaoh's daughter knew the decree of her father yet made arrangements for her new little man to be cared for by a Hebrew woman, who happened to be his own mother.

Like baby Moses, you and I have people in our lives who play key roles, ones that are so timely and necessary, and their compassion and kindness give us a glimpse of God's intentions and goodness toward each of us. They could include our parents, an aunt or uncle, a neighbor, a pastor, a teacher, or anyone who sees us as valuable and worthy of health and abundant life. As we process the broken pieces of our lives, we can search our stories and often find light bearers, those willing to carry the torch of love on our behalf.

Think of the women and men who played key roles in your own upbringing and write about their role and impact in the space on the following page. How did they represent the nature of God through their actions or words toward you?

As you contemplate God-sized dreams, remember that God is with you just as He was with Moses. He isn't joining you in the story of your life at the eleventh hour. He has been there from the beginning, arranging people of peace and grace to cross your path. He desires to be your Abba—your good Father who will keep you, hold you, and lead you as you dream beautiful dreams.

Offer a prayer of gratitude to God for His nearness—even when you didn't think He was near—and for His goodness—even when you didn't know He was the Giver of the good you received. If you want, write your prayer below.

DAY 4: YOUR PAST WON'T BREAK YOU

About a decade ago, I had a three-year stint of living in England. When I made the decision to move back to the States, I had no idea what I was going to do. With a broken heart and a spotty résumé, I felt as though my past choices and disappointments excluded me from God's best. Although I had big dreams, I could not see how He could work things out for my good because it felt like every big move I made somehow backfired. Things hadn't worked out as I would have hoped by that point, so I thought that disappointment would be my path in life. Surely my past experiences would squash any future hope of my dreams becoming reality. My broken endings left me believing lies about the nature of God and the plans He had for my life.

Our past experiences that have left us feeling shattered and hopeless can cause us to wonder how God could ever gather the broken fragments of our lives and piece them together to make something beautiful. For nearly all of us, our past is filled with ups and downs, heartache and loss. We can so easily feel disqualified from the good things of the future because of our past. According to society, we need to look the part and have a perfect track record; then we can pursue the big dreams beating in our hearts. But in God's kingdom, it's different. Regardless of our pasts, our missteps, and our broken endings, God still has a beautiful plan for our lives and invites us to partner with Him.

Describe a few past experiences that left you feeling hopeless or broken:

How did those experiences shape your view of God and your understanding of His plans for your life?

> Broken dreams, no matter how they happen, can cause us to question our worth, our direction, and even our right to embrace a God-sized dream. Many of us, myself included, sometimes feel that our plans are downright foolproof. Nothing will go wrong because we are always one step ahead and think everything through. It will all turn out rosy because life is rainbows and unicorns. Until it doesn't. . . .
>
> Despite the outcomes of our plan, God can redeem our broken dreams—replacing them with better ones—and set

You Were Born for This

> us on solid ground for the future. Even if those dreams have been dead for days, months, or years, the Lord is faithful to hear us when we call. Some of us may find ourselves in situations where we've lost more than we ever imagined at the hands of someone else's selfish choices. It can be easy to throw up a fist at God and ask Him why such a tragedy would happen; but on this side of heaven in a broken world where there is sin and suffering, unspeakable tragedy seems to find us in one way or another. Some say that you are either in a season of suffering, have just left a season of suffering, or are headed into a season of suffering. Suffering finds us all, and the sharp pain of shattered dreams can make us wonder if God has a plan at all—or if He does have a plan, if it is good.
>
> —*She Dreams*, pages 22-23

After his rescue by Pharaoh's daughter, we see nothing of Moses for years. I've always found it quite interesting that Pharaoh never disposed of Moses once he found out what his daughter was up to—especially since the child was returned to the princess after he was weaned, which would have meant that he was no longer an infant. Exodus 2:10 informs us, "Later, when the boy was older, his mother brought him back to Pharaoh's daughter, who adopted him as her own son. The princess named him Moses, for she explained, 'I lifted him out of the water.'" His adopted mama had compassion on his precious life.

Think of what would have happened if Pharaoh's daughter had not come down to the waters at the hour she did. The babe might have been destroyed in some way. But just as God called the heathen ruler Cyrus "His servant," so He used the pagan princess to deliver the child who was to become one of God's greatest heroes. For forty years Moses was cared for and educated as the son of Pharaoh's daughter, having all the privileges of a son of the royal court. Stephen declared, "Moses was learned in all the wisdom of the Egyptians, and was mighty in words and deeds" (Acts 7:22 NKJV). Surrounded with all the wealth and luxury of Pharaoh's court, Moses was taught to speak and write the Egyptian language correctly.[1] Moses, educated by Egyptians, would have been familiar with Egyptian rituals and customs. Despite the knowledge and training of a royal, we can see by his actions that Moses never forgot he was Hebrew. He was tender toward his people even though he led a life of luxury within Pharaoh's house.

Our key character in the Book of Exodus knew a thing or two about make-or-break moments. With the knowledge that he was an outsider living a privileged Egyptian life, the now-grown Moses visited his people, the enslaved Israelites forced to work under harsh conditions, and he broke. His heart sank and anger rose as He witnessed an Egyptian slave driver beating a Hebrew. So he intervened, and his actions had consequences that drastically altered his life's story.

Read Exodus 2:11-15 and describe the feelings you imagine Moses likely felt after this incident:

Moses' adopted royal family, the same ones who raised him and cared for him, now sought to end his life for his betrayal and murder. In one act, everything changed for Moses. I wonder if he even had a moment to say goodbye to his adopted mother? I wonder if he was able to visit his royal home one last time before word got out? However it ended, Scripture is clear that Moses lost everything he once knew as home. It was over. He left everything behind.

For a man who just murdered an Egyptian, I highly doubt Moses felt great about his days ahead. I suspect he felt like his past mistakes crushed any hopes or dreams that he once had. He was now a criminal on the run without any hope of returning to Egypt with open arms from Pharaoh or the royal family. Life would never be the same for him ever again.

Our past experiences can leave us, like Moses, feeling doubtful about our future hopes and dreams. We can be left broken and overwhelmed. Whether by the poor choices we made or the consequences of another's actions, we can feel defeated by our situation, unable to see how everything wrong could be made right.

Yet God in His goodness, mercy, and power isn't ever going to allow our past to disqualify us from our dreams, no matter how big or small they may be. The painful experiences we have under our belts aren't, in fact, the breaking of us but very well could be the making of us. They could be what lead us to the Father. They could be what cause us to cry out to the Dream Giver for help and healing. Our painful experiences of the past don't ever need to be swept under the rug and forgotten. We can bring them to the light. We can sift through them and find gems—lessons we wouldn't have learned otherwise. We can acknowledge how they have shaped us without allowing them to sink us.

From the past experiences you listed earlier (page 23), what did you learn about yourself? What did you discover that you didn't know before?

How have those past experiences shaped you as you have chased your dreams?

By God's grace we can become women who pursue their dreams not because we are perfect, flawless creatures but because we recognize that our God is a Redeemer; He does not disqualify us because of our past mistakes and failures. When we understand our past isn't the breaking of us but instead provides the makings of us, we can see that our God will partner with anyone for great and glorious plans. If he partnered with a murderer for the rescue of His people, He can partner with you and me. No matter what we've done, what we've encountered, or what we've lost, we are qualified for our dreams because the Dream Giver says so—not because of our track record. The God of all will partner with us for wild, audacious dreams as we live the lives we were created for!

DAY 5: DON'T SETTLE

When I sit down with my journal, Bible, and a steaming hot cup of coffee, I jot down my dreams in all caps with a bright blue pen. After I've written down my big dreams, I circle them to solidify my commitment to seeing them come to pass. I've done this for years. I circle those dreams again and again. They usually start out as only-by-God's-grace-could-this-happen kind of dreams. On the very next page of my journal, I outline what it will take for those dreams to come true, including my next steps, all the while trusting that the Lord will finish what He began in me. I usually run out of space and end up with all kinds of arrows pointing this way and that to connect the dots. I finish with prayer, begging the Lord to reveal Himself to me and give me wisdom because, heaven knows, I need it. I long, just as you do, for my dreams to become reality. I ache for the God-breathed dreams that occupy my thoughts to come true in just the way I desire, but nearly every time that isn't the case.

In almost every one of my dreams, I'm presented with an option to take an easier path—a choice to minimize the God-sized dream, allowing it to morph into something that sounds good but isn't exactly what I sensed the Lord was stirring in me; but because it seems like the path of least resistance, I am willing to give in. Do you ever find yourself doing that, too? Do you ever find yourself trading in God-sized dreams for dreams that provide a bit more comfort, security, or ease? It can happen to the best of us, and it certainly happened to the Israelites.

The Israelites cried out for freedom, and the reason they found themselves in a situation where freedom was now their heart cry was because they had settled for less than the God-sized dream that had been given to their ancestors Abraham, Isaac, and Jacob. They had taken the path of least resistance, and eventually they had paid for it in the form of oppression and slavery. They had traded their dreams, bit by bit, for a lesser god, and they didn't continue to trust the Lord with their lives. It didn't happen overnight but was a gradual progression ending with them crying out for rescue.

On Day 2 of this week we learned about the Israelite history in Egypt. Ten of Jacob's sons made their way to Egypt when they experienced a famine in Canaan, the same famine that Joseph predicted. When they arrived in Egypt to plead their case and ask for grain, they went before Pharaoh's second in command, Zaphenath-paneah (Genesis 41:45), whom they did not know was the brother they had hated and abandoned thirteen years earlier. These sons of Jacob came face-to-face with the brother they had abandoned and rejected who now held the power to feed them and their families. In his kindness that brother, Joseph, saved their tails from famine when he ensured a place in Egypt for them and their families.

Genesis 45:9-11 informs us of Joseph's instructions to his brothers once they realized that he was second in command over Egypt:

> ⁹"Now hurry back to my father and tell him, 'This is what your son Joseph says: God has made me master over all the land of Egypt. So come down to me immediately! ¹⁰You can live in the region of Goshen, where you can be near me with all your children and grandchildren, your flocks and herds, and everything you own. ¹¹I will take care of you there, for there are still five years of famine ahead of us. Otherwise you, your household, and all your animals will starve.'"

As we continue reading, we learn that Pharaoh was delighted to hear Joseph's family would be coming to Egypt. He made accommodations for them and offered them the finest that Egypt had to offer. He spared no expense as he invited them to make a home in Goshen.

Read Genesis 45:16-28 and Genesis 46:1-7 in your Bible, and complete the following:

¹⁴"So fear the Lord and serve him wholeheartedly. Put away forever the idols your ancestors worshiped when they lived beyond the Euphrates River and in Egypt. Serve the Lord alone. ¹⁵But if you refuse to serve the Lord, then choose today whom you will serve. Would you prefer the gods your ancestors served beyond the Euphrates? Or will it be the gods of the Amorites in whose land you now live? But as for me and my family, we will serve the Lord."

(Joshua 24:14-15)

List all that Pharaoh gave to Jacob and his family:

Was anyone in the Hebrew camp left behind in Beersheba?

Look again at Genesis 46:3-4. What was the promise God made to Jacob?

The Israelites settled into Goshen and enjoyed life in Egypt. Joseph lived until age 110 (Genesis 50:22), and Scripture indicates that after he died some of the people of God grew accustomed to more than just living in Egypt. We know they were dependent on Pharaoh's kindness for their food and land, but even more they grew accustomed to the Egyptians' gods.

Read Joshua 24:14-15 in the margin. What is Joshua referring to when addressing the Israelites?

The Israelites put their trust in Pharaoh for their land, food, and protection and even worshiped the false gods of Egypt. In Egypt, they traded their trust in God for their trust in Pharaoh. It was Pharaoh who became their provider, protector, and employer. It was the house of Pharaoh in whom they put their trust and, ultimately, it was the same house that oppressed and enslaved them. The Pharaoh mentioned in Exodus 1 did not show the same appreciation and kindness toward the Israelites that the pharaohs of the past had shown them. He knew nothing of Joseph and all he had done for Egypt.

As the Israelites withdrew their trust and worship of God to show allegiance to Pharaoh and worship the gods of Egypt, they put themselves at the mercy of Pharaoh, a mere man who did not have the best interests of the Israelites at heart. He was not the one who promised the Israelites that they would be a prosperous nation with many descendants and have a Promised Land of their own to call home. As the Israelites did indeed multiply, they became a threat, not an asset, and were enslaved by the very people in whom they had put their trust. Pharaoh wanted to remain in complete control, and with a growing Israelite population, he feared they would outnumber and overthrow him. So he lived out of fear, not freedom.

You and I crave comfort, security, food, and shelter just as the Israelites did. We long for things to go well for us and our families. Yet when we idolize the human giver of those comforts—when we give up on trusting God for the victory because what we have in front of us will suffice—we miss out on our promise; we miss out on our God-sized dreams. We trade trust in God and His plans for us for the modern-day pharaohs of this world. In the end, we trade more than just our trust; we trade our freedom to partner with the Dream Giver, and we find ourselves calling out for help just as the Israelites did when things do not go as planned (Exodus 2:23).

From your understanding of God's promises to the Israelites, why do you think the Israelites chose to worship the gods of Egypt?

Has there been a time when you've traded your God-sized dreams for hope in comforts or securities? If so, describe it briefly.

After the Israelites were enslaved and worked to the bone and their baby boys were being thrown into the Nile River in an attempt to erase their very existence, they cried out for help. God heard their cries and remembered His promise to their ancestors. He would rescue them just as He promised Jacob he would in Genesis 46:3-4.

God planned to deliver them, heal them, and give them the Promised Land. He, not Pharaoh, would be their King. He would be their Deliverer, not their slave driver. He would hold up His end of the promise despite the Israelites' choice to worship the gods of Egypt and place their trust and well-being in the hands of the king of Egypt.

In our lives, there almost always will be an easier way we can take, a path of least resistance; but God-sized dreams require us to follow after the Dream Giver and trust Him with our hearts, relationships, family, finances, and well-being. We can't worship God, trusting Him with our dreams, and also worship the pharaohs of this world. God requires our complete trust.

God longs to partner with you for wild dreams that invite you to give Him your trust and worship. In the space below, write your dreams in all caps and then circle them. Pray over each one, committing that dream and the path to reach it to the Lord.

GROUP SESSION GUIDE: WEEK 1

You Were Born for This

*The Dream Giver invites you to partner
with Him and trust Him for the impossible.
You are not disqualified. You are born to dream!*

Welcome/Prayer/Icebreaker (5–10 minutes)

Welcome to session 1 of *She Dreams*. Over the next six weeks we're going to find inspiration from the story of Moses as we discover and pursue our own God-given dreams; and best of all, we'll be making the journey together, encouraging and supporting one another all along the way. Take a moment to open with prayer, and then go around the circle and share something you dreamed of doing or becoming when you were a little girl.

Video (about 25 minutes)

Play the video segment for session 1, completing the following notes as you watch. Feel free to add notes about anything that resonates with you or that you want to be sure to remember.

—Video Notes—

Scriptures: *Exodus* 2:11-15; *Joshua* 24:14; *Leviticus* 17:7; *Ezekiel* 20:6-7

For each and every woman who has breath in her lungs, the Dream Giver calls her. She is not disqualified. She was _____ to _____.

When we settle, we don't lose out on just the dream; we lose out on who we are _____.

You Were Born for This   31

Our dreams aren't defined by our _____; they are defined by our _____.

God _____ _____ about the dreamers.

Group Discussion (20–25 minutes for a 60-minute session; 30–35 minutes for a 90-minute session)

Video Discussion

- Have you settled? Have you given up on your dreams or put them aside for now because of your past, your circumstances, or your season? How does it feel to know that God wants to partner with you for the impossible?

Personal Lessons Review and Discussion

Day 1

1. God's plans became the dreams of Moses' own heart—dreams that changed the course of his family and an entire nation. Like Moses' dreams, our own God-sized dreams change us and draw us to deeply depend on the Dream Giver, who will not leave us or forsake us.
    - How has pursuing a dream ever changed you (or someone you know or love)? How did it draw you (them) closer to God?

2. God invites us to trust Him as we dream impossible dreams that only He can bring to pass.
    - How do you sense God calling you to trust Him in this season? What could help you to grow your trust in God?

Day 2

1. If left longing for *too* long, the heart grows weary and struggles to keep dreaming and praying for resolve.
    - What longing in this season of life is unfulfilled? (page 15)
    - How has your unfulfilled longing affected your view of God? (page 15)

2. The Lord used poor Hebrew women to put His plans into motion in Moses' life. He was working even in the shadows of Exodus 1, positioning the right people in the right places to see the dreams of Israel's patriarchs—Abraham, Isaac, and Jacob—come to pass. And He does the same in our lives today.
   - Take turns reading Exodus 1 aloud. What role did the Hebrew midwives play, and how does this affect your understanding of God's plans? (page 17)
   - Review the story of Joseph on pages 17-18, and read aloud Genesis 50:22-26. How do we see God orchestrating a plan of deliverance for His people even before Moses took his first breath? How does this help you to trust that the Lord will be faithful to fulfill His dreams and plans in your life?

Day 3

1. Just as Moses had his momma, his sister, and his adoptive mother, we too have people in our lives who play key roles, ones that are so timely and necessary; and their compassion and kindness give us a glimpse of God's intentions and goodness toward each of us.
   - Who were the women and men who played key roles in your own upbringing? How did they represent the nature of God through their actions or words toward you? (pages 21–22)

Day 4

1. Moses took an action that had drastic consequences, altering his life's story. Like Moses, our past experiences can leave us broken and overwhelmed, feeling doubtful about our future hopes and dreams. But as Moses would discover, the painful experiences we have under our belts aren't, in fact, the breaking of us but very well could be the making of us.
   - Read Exodus 2:11-15. How do you imagine Moses felt after this incident? (page 25) How did his life change?
   - How have painful past experiences shaped you as you have chased your dreams? (page 26)

Day 5

1. We learned that the Israelites put their trust in Pharaoh for their land, food, and protection and even worshiped the false gods of Egypt. We crave comfort, security, food, and shelter just as they did. We long for things to go well for us and our families. Yet we miss out on God's promises and

dreams when we idolize anything other than God, trading trust in Him for the comforts and securities of this world.
   - From your understanding of God's promises to the Israelites, why do you think the Israelites chose to worship the gods of Egypt? (page 29)
   - Has there been a time when you've traded your God-sized dreams for hope in comforts or securities? If so, describe it briefly. (page 29)

2. God-sized dreams require us to follow after the Dream Giver and trust Him with our hearts, relationships, family, finances, and well-being. God requires our complete trust as we partner with Him for impossible dreams.
   - Why is complete trust necessary if we are going to partner with God? Is there an area where you struggle to trust God, and how might this be hindering what God wants to do in your life?

Becoming a Dreamer (10–15 minutes—90-minute session only)

Divide into groups of two to three and discuss the following:

- Share one or more of the wild, impossible, God-sized dreams you wrote on page 30. Dare to give it voice today in this group of safe and supportive co-dreamers.

Closing Prayer (5 minutes)

Close the session by sharing personal prayer requests and praying together. In addition to praying out loud for one another, ask God to help you trust Him more and more as you take steps toward the dreams He has planted in your hearts. Give thanks that your past or current circumstances do not define your dreams and that God promises to finish what he has started.

Week 2

God-Sized Dreams

Moses in Midian
(Exodus 2:15–4:17)

Your God-sized dreams will be bigger
than anything you could ever do on your own.

DAY 1: YOU DON'T SEE HOW IT COULD HAPPEN

This week as we continue diving into the story of Moses, we'll discover just how incredible and terrifying God's dreams for him really were. Last week we learned about the circumstances that surrounded him in the beginning of his life. Like Moses, we all have circumstances beyond our control, but that does not deter God from choosing us as partners in His redemptive work and plans. We were created for beauty and wonder, born for hope and peace. Each of us, no matter where we've come from or what we've done, can dream wild, seemingly impossible dreams with a God who loves us, cares for us, and invites us to be the very best versions of ourselves as we dream with Him.

> **Read chapter 3 of the *She Dreams* book, "Rewarding Life and Rewarding Work," noting below any insights or encouragement you gain from your reading:**

When have you felt disqualified from having or pursuing a God-sized dream because of circumstances beyond your control—including good things or blessings in your life (such as school, family, a job, etc.)?

The dreams in our hearts and the responsibilities we have are not intended to be at odds with each other but to work together to create a life we love. When we look to Mary, the mother of Jesus, the representative woman of Proverbs 31, and even Moses himself, we see individuals who were called by God yet still took care of what was already on their plates. It wasn't one or the other; they didn't pick. They chased after a full life with loved ones in tow. Now, I understand that certain seasons may demand more of us in one area than another; but the idea that we would lay down our God-inspired dreams because we have the blessing of a job or family or other obligations limits our understanding of a dreamer who is called by God for great and mighty purposes.

List your responsibilities in this current season of life (think about the categories of home/family, finances, work, church/community, education/training, etc.):

As you read in chapter 3, the archetypal Proverbs 31 woman is confident and strong, diligent and wise. She loves and cares for her family, has several interests, and is concerned for the disadvantaged in her community. As a representation of all women, she doesn't compartmentalize her life in an effort to keep balance but rather nurtures her family, pursues her dreams, puts her skills to work, and serves her community. She is purposed and has a full, vibrant life.

What encouragement do you find in this picture of a woman who serves her family and pursues her passions?

How can the pursuit of your dreams be a blessing to your loved ones, and how can your loved ones be a blessing to the pursuit of your dreams?

The Lord is familiar with all that is on your plate. He isn't unaware of your circumstances, obligations, commitments, and responsibilities. He sees every part of you—your gifts that may seem shelved, your strengths that may be underutilized, and your portion in this season. He does not see your dreams as being separate from your current life and commitments. He sees how it all can work together as you live the life you were created for. He is the Author of your life and the Giver of your dreams. You can trust Him with your commitments, your responsibilities, and your heart's deepest desires.

Offer a prayer of gratitude to the Lord for this season. However chaotic or peaceful it may be, give thanks to the Lord for His commitment to lead you in every aspect of your life. If you want, write your prayer below.

DAY 2: GOD STILL CAN

Yesterday we considered how the Proverbs 31 woman is a picture of a fabulous woman who loves and serves her family while pursuing her passions. As we discuss our dreams, it's good to remember that we all have responsibilities and commitments; and that is no reason to stop us from pursuing our dreams. We are built for a rewarding life and rewarding work.

Today we're diving back into the story of Moses and taking a look at what life looked like after he fled from Egypt. Remember, he left on bad terms with Pharaoh after killing an Egyptian and hiding him in the sand.

Read Exodus 2:11-15. Who knew what Moses had done, and what were their responses?

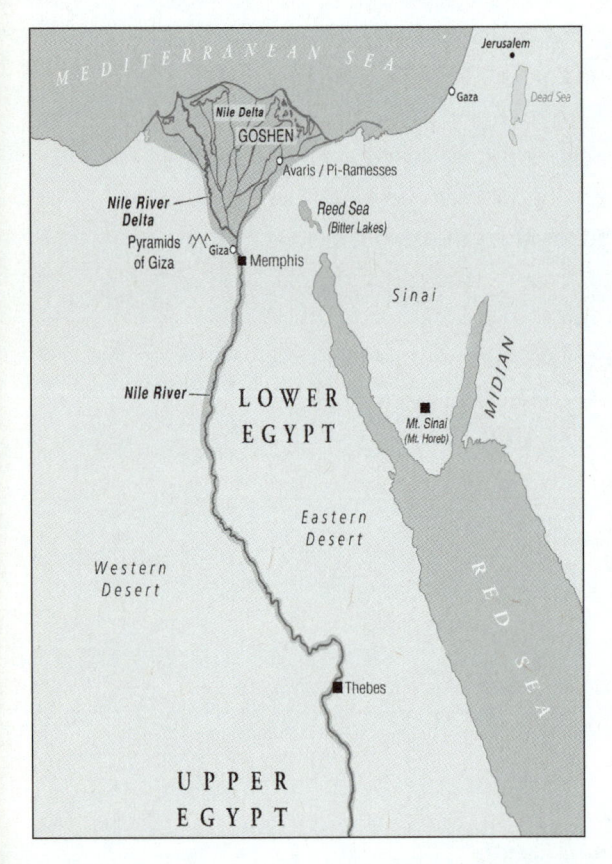

Where did Moses flee?

The Hebrew slaves knew what Moses had done, and it didn't take long for Pharaoh to find out what had happened as well. Moses' life was in danger because of the crime he had committed. By the laws of Egypt, he deserved death for his actions; and Pharaoh planned to enforce that law, putting to death a member of his own family. Pharaoh had no sympathy for Moses, who had felt the need to protect and defend his fellow man. Once Moses realized that Pharaoh was after him, he escaped to Midian.

As one source explains, if Moses had fled to Canaan and Syria, he would not have found refuge there because Pharaoh and the Hittite king had an arrangement that fugitives on

40 She Dreams

the route to Syria would be arrested and sent back to Egypt.[1] So Moses went instead to Midian. Life in Midian would have been vastly different than life in the luxurious palace of Egypt. In Egypt, Moses was royalty and had his every need met; but in Midian, he was a wanderer, a stranger in a foreign land.

Have you ever found yourself starting over in a new place or season and wondering how God could still make your dreams come to pass? If so, write about it briefly:

Years ago I thought that if I stepped away from the role I was in at the time, I would move further away from my dreams. I thought that if I stayed in my position—one I thought held opportunities that seemed to align with my dreams—then and only then would I be on my way to seeing my dreams become reality. How wrong I was. The Lord whispered to me in that full season to step away and follow Him. He made it clear that staying where I was would not be in alignment with His plan for my life, and that the dreams I had hoped and prayed for were not as vibrant as the ones He had for me. So I did it. I stepped away.

The conveniences and responsibilities I previously enjoyed were gone, and my life looked completely different. Once a full-time working woman, I transitioned to life at home with kids. At the time, I had a nine-month-old and a five-year-old. My days were filled with refilling sippy cups, reading with little ones on my lap, and bathing my precious boys. In the back of my mind I wondered if God knew that the dreams He had given me, the ones I held so dear, were still there. Although my season and life looked different than before, I was still a woman with great dreams; and I sure hoped the Lord saw me and had a plan.

The truth is, because of Jesus, because of God's love for us and the gift of His Son, we can partner with Him for dreams that defy the odds!

Write a statement declaring that God is still able to bring your dreams to pass even when your life changes and you can't see how He could work out the details:

Extra Insight

"The Midianites were descended from Midian, the fourth son of Abraham and his second wife Keturah, born in c.1819 BC (see Genesis 25:1-6). During Abraham's lifetime, Midian and his five brothers were sent 'to the east' (Genesis 25:6), and settled in territory to the east and south of the Dead Sea."[2]

God-Sized Dreams 41

It is by God's grace that we have life in Christ. You and I, dear friend, are "God's masterpiece...created...anew in Christ Jesus, so we can do the good things he planned for us long ago" (Ephesians 2:10). There is no clause in Scripture that states God will work out the good things He planned for us on our terms or in our way. It's God's way and His plan. I have come to believe the truth of Ephesians 2:10, and I've spoken it over others who needed a reminder that God can still work out His plans and bring the dreams in their hearts to pass. I've shared this passage again and again in prayer with other women—women who have experienced miscarriages, lost their jobs, or found themselves in the middle of a messy divorce; and with all of them I've declared that because of Jesus, our greatest gift from Father God, we too can believe we are God's masterpiece no matter what we've lost. We can know that we are created anew in Christ Jesus to do good things planned for us long ago. In a season of loss or change we may be tempted to worry that God can't work out the details of our dreams, but our sovereign God is good and with us every step of the way.

Moses is proof that even when it seems you are far away from the dream, God is at work. His choice to murder the Egyptian led him to drastically change the course of his life, fleeing from his home. In your life and mine, there can be times when everything changes and it appears we are farther away from the dream that burns in our heart. But remember this: God is not surprised when things or seasons change, bringing hard times. He is still the Dream Giver, and you can still dream even when the dream seems impossible.

Moses, an outlaw in Midian, was still called by God for great and mighty purposes. Moses, who had a bleeding heart for justice, wasn't disqualified from serving even though he was miles away from his oppressed brothers and sisters in Egypt. God planned to partner with Moses for the deliverance of the Israelites despite his track record. That was still God's dream for Moses, even though Moses didn't know it yet.

You and I can trust that God sees us, hears us, and knows our every thought. He is willing and able to partner with us despite whatever hurdles or losses we've experienced. Even when it seems that we are moving away from our dreams, God can meet us there to train us and mold us into women who can carry out those dreams in our hearts. A change in season might feel like one step backward; but friend, maybe it is actually forward movement. Maybe in your new season you will find that you are becoming the dreamer who can handle the size of the dream. Maybe God is working out the details for your good and your growth. Even when it seems that you are going in the wrong direction, you just may be walking smack-dab into the middle of your dream!

Meditate on Ephesians 2:10 and write it in your own words:

DAY 3: START SOMEWHERE

Read chapter 4 of the *She Dreams* book, "Tell Me Why," noting below any insights or encouragement you gain from your reading:

Extra Insight

The Midianites were descendants of Abraham and worshiped the true God. The name Reuel actually means "friend of God."[3]

Have you ever found yourself longing to start something new but, because you didn't feel that you had all the pieces in place, you stalled before you started?

> It can be overwhelming to think of how to start doing the very thing we wish to do. Yet we must start somewhere. God-sized dreams demand participation on our part. It's too easy to let months or years pass without taking the first step. But once we take the first step, we can march, shimmy, or hustle in the direction of our dreams. One two-step at a time. If we begin with the end in mind, we can remember that the pursuit is a process—one that is exciting and exhausting, costly and consuming.
>
> —*She Dreams*, pages 61-62

Moses' new start in Midian offers us some insights about the importance of just starting somewhere. Moses had a passion for justice, and he did not disown his passions in Midian. Even as he rested by the well upon his arrival, he saw an opportunity to defend and protect. From what we read in Exodus 2, it doesn't appear that he hesitated to use his voice or seemingly affluent position (made apparent by his royal threads) to serve the disadvantaged women at the well by ensuring they had a place and equal rights. His conviction and compassion led him to Reuel (or Jethro), the father of those he had defended and the priest of Midian. Reuel, who loved God and eventually loved Moses, was a source of encouragement and care for Moses. In his new start, Moses now had an ally, someone who accepted him and offered him kindness. Life in Midian would be easier because of the family Moses found through Reuel. Their relationship was a precious one—one we will see make an appearance much later in the story as well.

Moses "started somewhere" with conviction and compassion and then developed confidants. He shows us that when we start somewhere new or begin something new, we can look for allies—those who will cheer us on and offer us kindness, advice, and help. The quickest way for us to fail in any new venture or the pursuit of a dream is to assume we can do it all by ourselves. You and I need a support system, whether we are in a season of loss or in a season of new growth. We need help and encouragement for the journey ahead. As we develop confidants, we can allow our convictions and compassion to guide our actions just as Moses did.

How would you describe your confidants, convictions, and compassion in this season?

Confidants:

Convictions:

Compassion:

We may not have all the answers as we pursue the God-sized dreams in our hearts, but we can, like Moses, start somewhere. Even when it doesn't appear as glamorous as we'd hoped. We can start with confidants, convictions, and compassion. And we can trust that God is with us every step of the way, even when we don't see how He could work with such humble beginnings. God is faithful, and He is for us no matter what!

DAY 4: ME, GOD?

Have you ever found yourself shaking your head, and saying, "Me, God? You want me to chase that impossible dream that seems far too difficult to reach?

(You want me to start a business? You want me to run for office? You want me to foster a child? You want me to _____?) Well, God, you have got the WRONG GIRL! You can knock on someone else's door because I cannot, will not, do what you've asked me to do."

It's as if we are the lead character in the Dr. Seuss classic *Green Eggs and Ham*, thinking of different ways to say no to the offer of what, in the end, we will find to be delicious. Like the character in this story, we may find in the end that a yes is just what was needed. When we step up and out from the place we stand, we can find that God is waiting, ready for us to partner with Him for wild dreams.

Have you ever found yourself shaking your head when God asked you to do the impossible? If so, briefly describe the experience:

In today's passage you'll read of a moment that once again changed the trajectory of Moses' life—this time under much different circumstances. Rather than a murderous crime, this time it was a holy moment. Moses encountered the Divine, the One true God of Israel—the God who loved him, cared for him, and had plans that became his wildest dreams.

Read Exodus 3:3-22 and answer the following:

Why was Moses in the wilderness?

How do you think God had prepared Moses for that moment at the burning bush?

Why do you think Moses questioned God's plans in verse 11?

In our lives, we may not always see how God is preparing us for the journey ahead, but He most certainly is preparing us. We may not see how the demands of our lives prepare us for greater things ahead, but they do. Our preparation and training might not look like what we expected, but God knows exactly what He is doing. As I've said before, he does not waste a week, month, or year. Every season of our lives is to be enjoyed while simultaneously preparing us for the dreams ahead.

Moses, even though he didn't totally see it, was prepared by God his entire life to be the deliverer of the Israelites from Egypt. Living as a royal until he was forty, he was given the best education and opportunities. Then he started over in Midian, became a family man, learned to serve those around him, and took orders from the priest of Midian, his father-in-law, Reuel (or Jethro).

One commentator observes, "This first appearance of God to Moses found him tending sheep. This seems a poor employment for a man of his parts and education, yet he rests satisfied with it; and thus learns meekness and contentment, for which he is more noted in sacred writ, than for all his learning."[4] Moses wasn't a head of state when he was visited by the Divine. He was a lone man surrounded by sheep. After forty years in Egypt as a royal and forty years in Midian as a shepherd, Moses was ready for the next season God had for him. It was time; the moment had come for God to speak to Moses and let him in on the great plan of his life that would become the dream of his heart.

To get Moses' attention, God put on a show that would certainly catch Moses' eye. Nearby where Moses tended the flock, a bush was ablaze, and one might think that this bush—not a tree, but a bush common to the region—would have burned to a crisp in an instant.[5] As Moses took a closer look, he discovered that the bush, although consumed by fire, wasn't burning.

When and how has God done something to get your attention or catch your eye?

What do you think the burning bush might possibly symbolize or represent?

I've heard it said that the bush represented the condition of Israel. Consumed by fire, afflicted by their oppressors, but not burned. The Israelites continued to multiply and were not wiped out because God was with them.

Others say that just as the shrub flamed but did not burn up, so God's nature "is not wearied by action nor exhausted by bestowing, nor has its life any tendency towards ending or extinction."[6]

In any case, Moses, in God's timing, was ready to lead the Israelites out of Egypt; and although he questioned why God would choose him, we see that he listened to God's plan of redemption for Israel. God was aware of the strife and injustice the Israelites had endured; and in His infinite wisdom, God chose Moses to lead the way. Through a burning bush that didn't burn up, God invited Moses to partner with Him. Just as a fourth man was in the fire with Shadrach, Meshach, and Abednego in Daniel 3, God would be with Moses. He would not face the fiery trials and battles that the dream required on his own.

In one of the most painful seasons of my life, when I certainly felt the heat of the fire, I studied the Scriptures, found solace in the presence of God, and at times begged Him to make the road ahead as easy and carefree as possible. He did not answer those prayers where I pleaded for ease but, instead, allowed me to walk through fiery days, months, and years; and in the end I came out stronger, purified by the experience. The fire of my struggles never once consumed me. Because of God's goodness, I emerged from that season unsinged by the fire; and to the best of my ability I have been faithful to the plans He has for me.

You and I may find ourselves shaking our heads, wondering why God's plans and dreams for us make our lives more difficult than we expected, but God's plans for us are good: good for us, good for others, and glorious to God. We can trust that when He calls us and speaks over us, it is a sacred moment; we are on holy ground.

Offer a prayer to the God of Abraham, Isaac, and Jacob—the One who calls to you, the one who allows fiery trials in your life but will not allow you to be consumed because He will be with you. Offer Him your yes even when you may want to question why He is doing what He is doing in this season of your life. If you want, write your prayer below.

DAY 5: THE POWER AND PLANS OF GOD

> [13] But Moses protested, "If I go to the people of Israel and tell them, 'The God of your ancestors has sent me to you,' they will ask me, 'What is his name?' Then what should I tell them?"
>
> [14] God replied to Moses, "I AM WHO I AM. Say this to the people of Israel: I AM has sent me to you." [15] God also said to Moses, "Say this to the people of Israel: Yahweh, the God of your ancestors—the God of Abraham, the God of Isaac, and the God of Jacob—has sent me to you.
>
> This is my eternal name,
> > my name to remember for all generations."
> > (Exodus 3:13-15)

Expectant mothers often flip through a baby name book to read about the most popular or obscure names that folks are naming their kids and what those names mean. I remember borrowing several baby books from the library and earmarking pages based not only on a name but also on what it means. There is so much weight in a name. Countless times in scripture we are given someone's name along with the meaning of his or her name. Somehow the name carries meaning about what the person will do, an important life event, or what he or she will one day overcome. Often when a biblical character went through a major change or victory, he or she received a new name to mark the event or new season. The meanings of names carried weight in biblical times, and they still do in our world today.

Do you know the meaning of your name? If so, jot it down below. If not, you might look it up online.

While our names have meaning, none compare to the authority and power of God's name for Himself. Yesterday we dove into the desert with Moses as he witnessed a burning bush and heard the voice of God. Today we'll take a closer look at God's name for Himself and discover what He conveyed to Moses by sharing His name.

Read Exodus 3:13-15 in the margin. Why do you think Moses asked for the name of God?

What name did God give him? What thoughts do you have about what this name might mean?

When Moses heard all that God planned, he asked for God's name so he could tell the Israelites who had sent him. Moses knew that while the Israelites had made a home in Egypt, they had learned about and worshiped the false Egyptian gods. Each Egyptian god had a name, indicating the power that god held. So he prepared to answer the Israelites with a proper name of the God of their ancestors, one that would not be confused with any of the Egyptian gods they had become familiar with while in Egypt.

The God of Abraham, Isaac, and Jacob informed Moses to tell the Israelites that His name is "I AM." The God of Israel was saying that He is the self-existent One. The power and authority of His name would be an encouragement and reminder to Moses and the Israelites that He had not forgotten His promise to His people and would lead them to freedom because He was, is, and always will be supremely in charge of everything.

After revealing His plan and name to Moses, God promised that Moses would not go it alone. I AM would be with him. The unchanging, compassionate, faithful, and powerful God of Israel would be with him every step of the way. Moses would be a participant in the destiny of his life as he partnered with God.

In the next chapter, however, we see that Moses had major concerns about the dreams that God had for him.

Read Exodus 4 in your Bible and answer the following:

What concerns did Moses have about the plans of God?

What miracles did God perform for Moses, and why do you think He did this?

What might the staff of Moses represent?

Even though Moses had significant concerns about his role in the grand scheme of things, God, in His kindness, revealed to Moses just how powerful He truly was. His staff, most likely a simple shepherd's staff, would wield the power of God when necessary. To expose just a taste of His power, God turned the rod into a snake and back again.

God-Sized Dreams

One scholar comments on the significance of this, saying that "it intimated what and how pernicious his rod would be to the Egyptians.... When stretched forth by the hand of Moses or Aaron, it became a token to Israel of guidance, encouragement, and protection; but to Egypt, like the bite of the most poisonous serpent, it [warned of] desolating judgments."[7] Moses' staff would go with him throughout the exodus into the wilderness; and each time he would use it, the power and passion of God would be on display for all to see. It was a symbol of God's power.

In the same conversation between God and Moses at the burning bush, we witness another miracle as God healed the incurable ailment that appeared on Moses' hand. Scholars agree that this was most likely white leprosy (hence the white spots), which was incurable by the doctors of the day.[8]

God went on to explain what else Moses should do if Pharaoh didn't listen to his demands. Little did Moses know that Pharaoh would not only refuse to give in to Moses' demands; he would oppress the Israelites as never before. In his fear, anxiety, and doubt, Moses again voiced his uncertainty about God's plan to partner with Him for the deliverance of Israel. He was hesitant. Would you be too? I sure would!

> When we start pursuing the dreams in our hearts, we are often provided with ample opportunity to face our fears. When we start, with our limited knowledge but willing hearts, we are acutely aware of what we don't know and what we don't have....
>
> When fear keeps us from starting, convincing us that it won't work out or that we aren't gifted or skilled enough to dream God-sized dreams, it's helpful to play it out. What will it look like if our worst fears happen? What will it look like if our best attempts fail miserably? Could it be that the Lord will be with us, guiding us through victory and defeat, through the ups and the downs? Could it be that the He is ready and willing to lend strength and grow our character and capacity through our journeys? I believe so. Our God is faithful to lead us, support us, and fight for us. He is greater, much greater, than the worst fears we can imagine.
>
> —*She Dreams*, pages 68-69

In response to Moses' uncertainty, God made it crystal clear to him that Israel's redemption was His idea and would come by His hand; victory would be theirs. Yet Moses still didn't feel he could speak on behalf of God. God was incredibly patient and understanding with Moses—as He is with us. Praise be!

God heard Moses and was kind enough to allow his brother, Aaron, to speak on his behalf.

Moses was aware of his insecurities, just as we are; but let us never forget that our insecurities will not stop God from choosing us as His partners for His divine work. We may disqualify ourselves, but God does not. Just as God allowed Aaron to be the mouthpiece to the people of Israel, God compassionately allows others to participate in our dreams in ways that accomplish things we could not do on our own. Even before Moses made his way back to Egypt, it's clear that God had people in place to support Moses as he pursued the dreams God had placed in his heart.

From today's passage, we've learned that the power and plans of God are unstoppable! God is good and kind and acts on behalf of His children. He partners with ordinary people like you and me to usher in His divine plans—ones we could never orchestrate or accomplish on our own. He has the power to fulfill His plans, and He is faithful to those who call on Him. To God be the glory!

Complete the sentences below, acknowledging the faithfulness of God to partner with you in your dreams.

Although I might not always feel qualified, I know God is

_____.

Although I don't always see how things can work out, I know God is

_____.

GROUP SESSION GUIDE: WEEK 2

God-Sized Dreams

Dreams are born in dissonance.
When our hearts break for what breaks God's own heart,
that's where God-sized dreams come to life!

Welcome/Prayer/Icebreaker (5–10 minutes)

Welcome to session 2 of *She Dreams*. We have been looking to the story of Moses as we discover and pursue our own God-given dreams, finding inspiration through the Scriptures and our fellow dreamers. You'll need the encouragement of this group as dreams rise up and come alive. Take a moment to open with prayer, and then go around the circle and share a ministry or mission that you are passionate about or an injustice that breaks your heart.

Video (about 25 minutes)

Play the video segment for session 2, completing the following notes as you watch. Feel free to add notes about anything that resonates with you or that you want to be sure to remember.

—Video Notes—

Scriptures: Exodus 2:15c-17; 3:11-12

Dreams are born in the _____.

Not only are dreams born in the dissonance; they are _____ by it.

Vision for the dream is important, but the _____ we develop is imperative.

We have to move _____ even before we can see any _____.

Group Discussion (20–25 minutes for a 60-minute session; 30–35 minutes for a 90-minute session)

Video Discussion

- What is your God-sized dream, and what is the dissonance that seems to be getting in the way?

Personal Lessons Review and Discussion

Day 1

1. Like Moses, we all have circumstances beyond our control, but that does not deter God from choosing us as partners in His redemptive work and plans. Each of us, no matter where we've come from or what we've done, can dream wild, seemingly impossible dreams with a God who loves us, cares for us, and invites us to be the very best versions of ourselves as we dream with Him.
   - When have you felt disqualified from having or pursuing a God-sized dream because of circumstances beyond your control—including good things or blessings in your life (such as school, family, a job, etc.)? (page 38)

2. The dreams in our hearts and the responsibilities we have are not intended to be at odds with each other but to work together to create a life we love.
   - How might dreams and responsibilities be at odds with each other?
   - Review your thoughts about the Proverbs 31 woman from page 39. What encouragement do you find in this picture of a woman who serves her family and pursues her passions?

Day 2

1. On the run for committing a crime, Moses fled to Midian. Life in Midian would have been vastly different from life in the luxurious palace of Egypt. In Egypt, Moses was royalty and had his every need met; but in Midian, he was a wanderer, a stranger in a foreign land.
   - When have you found yourself starting over in a new place or season and wondering how God could still make your dreams come to pass? (page 41)

2. There is no clause in Scripture that states God will work out the good things He planned for us on our terms or in our way. It's God's way and His plan.

- Read Ephesians 2:10. How does this passage encourage us regarding God's timing and our dreams?
- When and how has God's timing surprised you?

Day 3

1. Moses didn't stall out in his dream pursuit while in Midian, even when he was basically starting over. Instead he offers us some insight about just starting somewhere. Moses "started somewhere" with conviction and compassion and then developed confidants. He shows us that when we start somewhere new or begin something new, we can look for allies—those who will cheer us on and offer us kindness, advice, and help.
    - Take turns reading Exodus 2. How do these verses show a starting over for Moses?
    - Refer to what you wrote on page 44 about your confidants, convictions, and compassion. What insights do your comments reveal about your support system, your beliefs, and your passionate concern for other people or causes?

Day 4

1. In our lives, we may not always see how God is preparing us for the journey ahead, but He most certainly is preparing us. We may not see how the demands of our lives prepare us for greater things ahead, but they do. Our preparation and training might not look like what we expected, but God knows exactly what He is doing.
    - Take turns reading Exodus 3:3-22. How do you think God had prepared Moses for that moment at the burning bush? (page 45)
    - When and how has God done something to get your attention or catch your eye? (page 46)
    - What do you think the burning bush might possibly symbolize or represent? (page 46)

Day 5

1. God promised that Moses would not go it alone. I AM, God's very name and presence, would be with him. The unchanging, compassionate, faithful, and powerful God of Israel would be with him every step of the way. Moses would be a participant in the destiny of his life as he partnered with God.

- Read Exodus 3:13-15. Why do you think Moses asked for the name of God? What name did God give him? (page 48)
- What have you learned is significant about the name God gave Moses?

2. Moses was aware of his insecurities, just as we are; but let us never forget that our insecurities will not stop God from choosing us as His partners for His divine work. We may disqualify ourselves, but God does not.
    - Refer to Exodus 4. What concerns does Moses have about his ability to perform the task to which God has called him?
    - When have you felt less than qualified to complete a task God has called you to? What do you know to be true about God when you feel unqualified and can't see how things will work out? (Refer to your responses on page 51.)

Becoming a Dreamer (10–15 minutes—90 minute session only)

Divide into groups of two to three for the following:

- Take some time to name aloud fears, excuses, and obstacles that keep you from forward motion toward your God-sized dreams. When we name fears, we bring them into the light and they lose their power to keep us paralyzed.

Closing Prayer (5 minutes)

Close the session by sharing personal prayer requests and praying together. In addition to praying out loud for one another, ask God to help you start somewhere. Give thanks for where you've been and what you've learned along the way. Ask God to use everything for His good as you take it all with you into God's great future.

Week 3

Fighting for the Dream

Moses in Egypt
(Exodus 4:18–12:32)

Dreams require our constant participation
as we trust the Lord for the victory.

DAY 1: DO WHAT IS IN YOUR POWER TO DO

Read chapter 5 of the *She Dreams* book, "Haters Gonna Hate," noting below any insights or encouragement you gain from your reading:

In this chapter we read about haters who never get on board with our dreams or who stand in opposition to what God is doing within and through us, as well as the importance of having supporters who encourage us. Later this week we will take a closer look at Moses' chief hater, Pharaoh, but today I want to briefly acknowledge the supporters that Moses had in his corner. In the chapter we consider Moses' brother, Aaron, who spoke for Moses before Pharaoh and was a companion throughout the journey in the wilderness. We learn in Exodus 4 that Moses' father-in-law, Jethro (referred to as Reuel in Exodus 2), played a supportive role as well.

Read Exodus 4:18 in the margin. Why do you think Moses asked his father-in-law for permission to return to Egypt, and what was his response?

So Moses went back home to Jethro, his father-in-law. "Please let me return to my relatives in Egypt," Moses said. "I don't even know if they are still alive."

"Go in peace," Jethro replied.
(Exodus 4:18)

Fighting for the Dream   57

With this support and blessing from his father-in-law, followed by confirmation from God in verse 19, Moses set off for Egypt. From verses 24-26 we learn that Moses' son had not been circumcised according to God's covenant with Abraham (Genesis 17:9-14), and Moses nearly lost his life for it; so Zipporah used a rock to circumcise her son. Not exactly a great start back to Egypt, but God did spare Moses' life after the circumcision of his son.

This may seem like a confusing incident to us, and I encourage you to look into what scholars have to say about it; but for our purposes, suffice it to say that integrity and obedience matter as we pursue our God-sized dreams. The Lord sees us and knows us as we are. If He is partnering with us to chase after big dreams, we can't shift into cruise control on the journey.

In the final verses of Exodus 4 we see that Moses met Aaron in the wilderness and brought him up to speed on the plan. Then the two of them returned to Egypt and called all of the elders of Israel together.

Here's the bottom line for us: We need to do what is in our power to do. If it's asking for permission from the Jethros in our lives, then we must ask. If it's taking care of affairs that should have already been taken care of, then we can get to it. If it's gathering those who will be partners in our destiny, as Moses and Aaron did with the elders of Israel, then let us gather. Whatever our next steps may be, we can move forward with integrity and obedience. Though opposition will find us, we will be able to handle any haters that lie ahead if we stand firm in who God has called us to be and rely on the support of others!

What next steps that are within your reach and power to do can you take toward seeing your dream become reality?

DAY 2: HATERS VS. HELPERS

Our dreams come in all shapes and sizes, demand our participation, and usually stretch us in ways we didn't even know we could be stretched! That's just what dreams do; but praise God that He is with us every step of the way, being faithful to lead us even when the going gets tough. This week we see that the going certainly got tough for Moses. Things heated up when he heeded the call of God and made his way back to Egypt. He encountered opposition from Pharaoh and fought in big ways for the dream God had placed on his heart.

Like Moses, we face challenges that test our courage, conviction, and trust in God, the Dream Giver. I would love to say that I've never found myself in a situation where I had to hush the haters and dig deep to display courage in a way that exhausted me, but that would be a boldfaced lie because this life is hard and our wild, God-sized dreams don't come easy. In fact, the dreams God has placed within us usually require a fight.

Pop star Taylor Swift sang that when the haters hate, "Baby I'm just gonna shake, shake, shake, shake, shake / I shake it off, I shake it off."[1] The catchy tune was a hit; and regardless of how you feel about Miss Swift, she may be on to something. In my own life I've found that even though I can't control how people treat me, I can choose how I treat those who oppose my dreams; and I can choose to stand my ground no matter how hard it may be. It's when haters come against our dreams or personhood that we are faced with the opportunity to either receive the offense or disrespect they're offering or stand our ground, even more convinced of what God is doing in and through us.

Today we'll discover the role and impact of a hater and determine how we can handle our own haters.

We've seen that even before arriving in Egypt, Moses' journey was full of ups and downs; and as he prepared to go before Pharaoh, he garnered the support of the Israelite leaders. Once in Egypt, Moses made his way to meet with the chief oppressor of the Israelites, Pharaoh; and Moses' request to hold a festival in the wilderness wasn't exactly met with a warm welcome.

Read Exodus 5 in your Bible. How did Pharaoh oppose Moses?

Why do you think Pharaoh increased the workload of the Israelites? What message was he sending to Moses and Aaron by his actions?

How do you think Moses and Aaron felt after their encounter with Pharaoh?

The effects of those who oppose our dreams can vary, but it nearly always has a negative impact that can cause us to question if what we believe in matters—or worse, if we what we are fighting for is even worth the fight. The actions of those who oppose our dreams can deter us or make us more determined. Let's see what happened with Moses.

Read Exodus 6:1-13 below:

¹**Then the Lord told Moses, "Now you will see what I will do to Pharaoh. When he feels the force of my strong hand, he will let the people go. In fact, he will force them to leave his land!"**

²**And God said to Moses, "I am Yahweh—'the Lord.' ³I appeared to Abraham, to Isaac, and to Jacob as El-Shaddai—'God Almighty'—but I did not reveal my name, Yahweh, to them. ⁴And I reaffirmed my covenant with them. Under its terms, I promised to give them the land of Canaan, where they were living as foreigners. ⁵You can be sure that I have heard the groans of the people of Israel, who are now slaves to the Egyptians. And I am well aware of my covenant with them.**

⁶**"Therefore, say to the people of Israel: 'I am the Lord. I will free you from your oppression and will rescue you from your slavery in Egypt. I will redeem you with a powerful arm and great acts of judgment. ⁷I will claim you as my own people, and I will be your God. Then you will know that I am the Lord your God who has freed you from your oppression in Egypt. ⁸I will bring you into the land I swore to give to Abraham, Isaac, and Jacob. I will give it to you as your very own possession. I am the Lord!'"**

⁹**So Moses told the people of Israel what the Lord had said, but they refused to listen anymore. They had become too discouraged by the brutality of their slavery.**

¹⁰**Then the Lord said to Moses, ¹¹"Go back to Pharaoh, the king of Egypt, and tell him to let the people of Israel leave his country."**

¹²**"But Lord!" Moses objected. "My own people won't listen to me anymore. How can I expect Pharaoh to listen? I'm such a clumsy speaker!"**

¹³**But the Lord spoke to Moses and Aaron and gave them orders for the Israelites and for Pharaoh, the king of Egypt. The Lord commanded Moses and Aaron to lead the people of Israel out of Egypt.**

(Exodus 6:1-13)

How did God encourage Moses after his encounter with Pharaoh?

Moses told the people of Israel what God planned to do; but under the weight of their slavery, they buckled. Understandably, their discouragement kept them from believing the good plans Moses shared. Moses explained to God how the Israelites wouldn't listen, and God instructed Moses to return to Pharaoh. I don't know about you, but the idea of returning for a second round in the ring with my hater isn't exactly what I would want to do! But with God as our King and our source of strength, we can stand back up, march back in, and do what God has called us to do.

Has someone discouraged you in your journey? If so, how has that impacted the way you see your dream?

> Haters cause us to ask the question, "Why don't you like me? What's your problem with me?" Their actions pinch a nerve that proves painful—so painful at times that we can't get our minds off of it. As we question ourselves, let us go to the throne of God and be reminded that we are loved. We are enough. We are gifted. We are called. We are purposed. A holy God leads us. We are built for the glory of God. We are living our story, one full of highs and lows, sacrifices and gains. Like Moses, may we be dreamers who will not stop for those who hate. Never. Ever.
>
> —*She Dreams*, page 77

Although haters may test your patience or take the wind right out of your sails, we can go back to the throne room of God and invite the Lord to be our leader, our encourager, and our victory giver! He is faithful to draw near; and if we listen, His voice will be louder than anyone who opposes our dreams. Amen!

In the space below, write a declaration affirming that even though some people may oppose what the Lord is stirring in you, by God's grace and leading you can carry on:

DAY 3: ONE STEP AT A TIME

Read chapter 6 of the *She Dreams* book, "Good Ole Days," noting below any insights or encouragement you gain from your reading:

Today you read about the importance of savoring your days. You and I may have big dreams and eager hearts to see our dreams become reality, but each day is a gift—one to savor. We may have a season when we accomplish more or don't gain the ground we expected, but in both seasons there is progress to praise. In both seasons God is present and working with us, even if it isn't as glamorous as we thought it might be.

Don't get me wrong: it would be wonderful if everything happened in just the way we wanted it to. Wouldn't it be just fabulous if God's timing aligned with our timing? While that would be just peachy, that is not often the case. But God is always with us, leading us one step at a time—in His time. As we learn to believe and trust Him, He is stretching and growing us into strong women of faith and courage.

When have you felt discouraged because plans didn't go according to your time line, and how did that experience affect your view of God and His time line?

As you discovered from chapter 6, I am no stranger to discouragement when it comes to my dreams being delayed or deferred. I may wonder where and how God is working, but the truth is that although I don't know exactly what the Lord is planning for me, I do know it is good. Very good. His ways are unlike mine, and that's okay. He is good at being God!

Read Isaiah 55:8-9 in the margin. How is this good news for a dreamer?

"My thoughts are nothing like your thoughts," says the LORD.
"And my ways are far beyond anything you could imagine. For just as the heavens are higher than the earth, so my ways are higher than your ways and my thoughts higher than your thoughts."
(Isaiah 55:8-9)

It is good news that the Lord takes our whole lives into account and has our best interests at heart. It is good news that He sees all, knows all, and loves us. We might not see how things will work out or how the dream may come to pass, but even now the Lord is at work; and we're probably gaining more ground than we think we are as we pursue the dream! You may be living through your good ole days right this minute, when God is stretching and molding you into the woman who can handle the days ahead.

What progress toward your dream have you already seen in your life?

Stop! Stop this very minute and celebrate what God has done! You may not be where you want to be, but you aren't where you used to be. The dream doesn't magically happen overnight. It happens with one good choice after another, one

Fighting for the Dream   63

prayer after another, and one step after another. Offer a prayer of praise to God for all He has brought you to thus far. If you want, write your prayer below.

DAY 4: HELPERS

You know those friends who are there for you no matter what? Not just the casual ones you grab a coffee with once in a while; I'm talking about the ones who sit across from you at the kitchen table, pour you a second cup of coffee, help you plan out your next steps, and offer their strengths. You know the ones? Those who stand by you, hold your hand, and battle alongside you as you fight for your dreams. Those friends are the helpers. Heaven knows we need the helpers!

Yesterday in chapter 6 of the *She Dreams* book, you read about how I started Sip and Savor Bible study with God leading me one step a time. He graciously brought others into the story who could help make Sip all that it is today. However, before Sip was even a dream, before I approached my friend, Chef Derek, about hosting Bible study in his space, and before all of the gifted women hopped on board to help make it happen, I sat at my kitchen table across from Chef Derek and his wife—my dear friends who were about to open their first restaurant, The Table—with a yellow legal pad and pen in my hands. We talked for hours about what people The Table would serve and what its purpose would be. Until it read perfectly, we worked together to craft the ideal mission statement that would be their guiding light for years to come.

To the best of my ability, I connected with local influencers who could spread the word about the restaurant's opening, and I had the honor of writing a story in a local magazine about its mission and the man behind it all. I did what I could with the strengths and gifts I had to serve my friends as they opened up their dream establishment. Little did I know that just a few months later the restaurateur and chef would come alongside my dream in a big way by allowing me to host Bible study in his space and creating dishes to serve women ready to feast on the Word and fine fare.

Isn't it a gift when others believe in you and your dreams? With more than a word of encouragement, they leverage their gifts, strengths, and resources to see your dreams come to pass. It's a great gift when others lock arms with you and me to see us go farther and faster toward the God-sized dreams beating in our hearts. Like Aaron did for Moses, they lend their strength to us so we can carry on with pursuing the dreams God has placed within us.

Our main man Moses had haters, no doubt about that; but as we've seen, he also had helpers. He had those who journeyed alongside him, believed in what God was doing within him, and stood with him when the going got incredibly tough. The same is true of us. We may encounter haters, but we also have helpers who journey alongside us one step at a time to see our dreams become reality.

Read the passages below and answer the questions that follow:

¹⁰But Moses pleaded with the Lord, "O Lord, I'm not very good with words. I never have been, and I'm not now, even though you have spoken to me. I get tongue-tied, and my words get tangled."

¹¹Then the Lord asked Moses, "Who makes a person's mouth? Who decides whether people speak or do not speak, hear or do not hear, see or do not see? Is it not I, the Lord? ¹² Now go! I will be with you as you speak, and I will instruct you in what to say."

¹³But Moses again pleaded, "Lord, please! Send anyone else."

¹⁴Then the Lord became angry with Moses. "All right," he said. "What about your brother, Aaron the Levite? I know he speaks well. And look! He is on his way to meet you now. He will be delighted to see you. ¹⁵Talk to him, and put the words in his mouth. I will be with both of you as you speak, and I will instruct you both in what to do. ¹⁶Aaron will be your spokesman to the people. He will be your mouthpiece, and you will stand in the place of God for him, telling him what to say. ¹⁷And take your shepherd's staff with you, and use it to perform the miraculous signs I have shown you."

(Exodus 4:10-17)

²⁷It was Moses and Aaron who spoke to Pharaoh, the king of Egypt, about leading the people of Israel out of Egypt.

²⁸When the Lord spoke to Moses in the land of Egypt, ²⁹he said to him, "I am the Lord! Tell Pharaoh, the king of Egypt, everything I am telling you." ³⁰But Moses argued with the Lord, saying, "I can't do it! I'm such a clumsy speaker! Why should Pharaoh listen to me?"

(Exodus 6:27-30)

¹Then the Lord said to Moses, "Pay close attention to this. I will make you seem like God to Pharaoh, and your brother, Aaron, will be your prophet. ²Tell Aaron everything I command you, and Aaron must command Pharaoh to let the people of Israel leave his country. ³But I will make Pharaoh's heart stubborn so I can multiply my miraculous signs and wonders in the land of Egypt. ⁴Even then Pharaoh will refuse to listen to you. So I will bring down my fist on Egypt. Then I will rescue my forces—my people, the Israelites—from the land of Egypt with great acts of judgment. ⁵When I raise my powerful hand and bring out the Israelites, the Egyptians will know that I am the Lord."

⁶So Moses and Aaron did just as the Lord had commanded them. ⁷Moses was eighty years old, and Aaron was eighty-three when they made their demands to Pharaoh.

⁸Then the Lord said to Moses and Aaron, ⁹"Pharaoh will demand, 'Show me a miracle.' When he does this, say to Aaron, 'Take your staff and throw it down in front of Pharaoh, and it will become a serpent.'"

¹⁰So Moses and Aaron went to Pharaoh and did what the Lord had commanded them. Aaron threw down his staff before Pharaoh and his officials, and it became a serpent! ¹¹Then Pharaoh called in his own wise men and sorcerers, and these Egyptian magicians did the same thing with their magic. ¹²They threw down their staffs, which also became serpents! But then Aaron's staff swallowed up their staffs. ¹³Pharaoh's heart, however, remained hard. He still refused to listen, just as the Lord had predicted.

(Exodus 7:1-13)

Describe the strengths of Moses:

Describe the strengths of Aaron:

How would you describe the friendship between Moses and Aaron?

How would you describe Aaron's role in the Exodus?

Aaron's kindness, boldness, and sacrificial spirit served Moses and all of the Israelites as he bravely stepped into the role God had for him. Moses and Aaron were brothers and comrades—and their sister, Miriam, was a supportive part of their leadership team as well. They had one another's backs and lent their strengths to one another as they pursued the dream of freedom for Israel. Moses was never left to fight for the dream on his own; he had Aaron and Miriam and the Dream Giver Himself, Father God.

In our own lives, we have those who are helpers—those who journey alongside us, weep with us, and serve us in ways that move us toward the dreams God has for us. They may not be rock stars in the eyes of others, but we could not, and often would not, chase the dream without them at our side. They are the ones who listen to us as we share about our convictions, passions, and hopes. They offer their support, not just their opinions, to help us move forward. They also are usually the ones who lovingly point out our blind spots, those things we haven't anticipated, as we trot along on the journey.

Define or describe a helper in your own words:

As you pursue your dream, what would the role of a helper look like in your life?

List below some of the helpers in this season of your life and the ways they have helped you pursue your dream:

⁹Two people are better off than one, for they can help each other succeed. ¹⁰If one person falls, the other can reach out and help. But someone who falls alone is in real trouble. ¹¹Likewise, two people lying close together can keep each other warm. But how can one be warm alone? ¹²A person standing alone can be attacked and defeated, but two can stand back-to-back and conquer. Three are even better, for a triple-braided cord is not easily broken.
(Ecclesiastes 4:9-12)

As one woman, there is a good chance you can't do it all; you need the gifts and abilities of others to see your dream come to pass. Like Moses, we can be completely honest with God about our insecurities and weaknesses and ask Him to send us helpers to aid us on our journey toward our dreams.

Read Ecclesiastes 4:9-12 in the margin. Why is it necessary to have a helper as you chase your dreams?

Is there someone in your world whose help you need in order to advance to the next step of your dream?

I wouldn't be who I am today without the helpers, the companions who never give up on what God is doing in my life. They are the ones who lend their strengths, skills, and resources to me as I chase after the dream God has placed deep in my heart. I am forever thankful for my helpers and do my best to show them my gratitude, because my experiences with them aren't merely transactional; they are relational and transformational. The gifts they offer are reminders that God is with me, offering provision for the vision.

As you think of the helpers in your life, be sure to thank them for all they've done and are doing to help as you chase your dreams.

DAY 5: LET MY PEOPLE GO

As we wrap up our last day this week, let's take a peek at Moses' commitment to freedom for the people of Israel. Yesterday we left off with Moses and Aaron working together to go before Pharaoh and demand freedom for God's people. Since Pharaoh, with a hardened heart, did not give in to the demands that Moses and Aaron made, terrible plagues hit Egypt. The plagues, wild occurrences of nature ordained by a supernatural God, proved that He was in control—not Pharaoh or the gods of Egypt—and that He would not stop until the dream of freedom was a reality for His beloved people.

Pharaoh waffled back and forth as he gave permission to Moses for the Israelites to leave and then refused to let them leave, and the Egyptian people suffered because of Pharaoh's hardened heart. But we'll see that no obstacle could derail Moses' God-given dream.

Let's walk through the ten plagues and consider Pharaoh's response to each.

Look up each Scripture and complete the chart:

Scripture	Plague	Description	Pharaoh's Response
7:14-24	Water into blood		
8:1-15	Frogs		
8:16-19	Gnats		
8:20-32	Flies		
9:1-7	Livestock		
9:8-12	Boils		
9:13-35	Hail		
10:1-20	Locusts		

Extra Insight

According to Egyptian history, after a pharaoh died, a mythical god would weigh his heart to see how just or unjust he was. If he was just, it would be lighter; if he was unjust, it would have been hard and heavy. If his heart was heavy and hardened, the belief was that he would be gobbled up by a terrifying beast and never become a deity.[2]

Fighting for the Dream

10:21-29	**Darkness**		
11:1–12:33	**Death of Firstborn**		

When you study the plagues that hit Egypt, do they seem mystical? Completely unrealistic? However they strike you, there is more than meets the eye here.

Scholars have explained the significance of some of the plagues as they relate to the gods of Egypt, showing how some even made a satirical statement about the ineffectiveness of the Egyptian gods. Author Adam Hamilton draws on this scholarship to present this helpful summary in his book *Moses: In the Footsteps of the Reluctant Prophet*:

> The first plague, turning the Nile and the other waters to blood so they could not give life, was a way of showing God's control over the Nile. In Egyptian mythology the god of the Nile was called Hapi.... Hapi was crucial to sustaining of life in Egypt. But in this first plague, the God of Israel overpowered Hapi, the god of the Nile.
>
> In the second plague, the frogs climbed out of the river and became a nuisance. Heket was a goddess in Egypt portrayed as a frog....
>
> Likewise, the death of the cattle in the fifth plague may have indicated God's power over the Egyptian goddess Hathor, who was often portrayed as a cow.
>
> Where we see satire most dramatically is in the ninth plague, when the sun was blotted out. Remember that Ramesses' and Moses' names had a common root: Moses meant "son of," which without a prefix meant Son of No One; while Ramesses' name meant Son of Ra (Ra being the sun god). In this battle between the eighty-year-old stuttering Son of No One and the powerful Son of Ra the sun god, Moses' God, Yahweh, defeated Pharaoh's sun god, causing utter darkness.[3]

The God of Moses would outshine the gods of Egypt for His glory. Moses, the Israelites, and the Egyptians witnessed the powerful, miraculous, sovereign God of the Israelites.

We've seen that Moses demanded Pharaoh let his people go, but Pharaoh redacted his promise and chose to oppress them instead, proving to be an obstacle for Moses and the Israelites.

> I can't even begin to imagine the deep discouragement Moses felt as Pharaoh messed with his head. Like Moses, you and I can easily feel as though victory is just around the corner yet meet discouragement again and again and again. In the midst of God's activity we are saddened to see that what we want so badly still appears to be out of reach. We've done everything we felt prompted to do, but the victory is out of sight once more. The dream seems too far away to grasp. In those moments it can seem that things will never bend our way. Yet the King is still working. The Lord is orchestrating our growth in ways we never could achieve on our own. Still, you and I both know it can be a painful and heart-wrenching journey even when we trust the Lord for the victory.
>
> —*She Dreams*, page 105

What real or potential obstacles stand in the way of your dream becoming reality?

It's vital to identify the obstacles that stand in the way of your dream, those things that may derail or test you on the journey, causing discouragement. In my own life, identifying the obstacles of a dream makes me more alert and attentive to what it will take to see the dream come to pass. In those times when I feel as though my dream will never become a reality, I've leaned into the Lord and listened for His instructions. He is faithful to instruct me, lead me, and encourage me to chase the dream no matter what, because the Dream Giver is greater than any obstacle.

In the face of Moses' obstacles, God was faithful to lead and encourage him every step of the way. After eight of the plagues had come and gone, the Lord instructed Moses to prepare for Passover.

Read Exodus 12:1-30 in your Bible. In the space below, outline the instructions God gave Moses for Passover:

What was the purpose of the Passover? (See Exodus 12:5, 21-28.)

What foreshadowing do you notice in the use of an unblemished lamb? (See 1 Peter 1:19.)

Why were the Israelites instructed to dress for travel while they ate the Passover meal? (See Exodus 12:11, 17, 33.)

According to the passage, what did the Festival of Unleavened Bread represent? (See Exodus 12:17, 33-34.)

The Passover festival, according to Scripture, would be an annual holiday to honor the night the Lord spared the Israelites as He "passed over" the homes of those who followed the detailed instructions to keep them from death. Every firstborn male would taste the sting of death if someone had not painted the doorframes of their homes with the blood of an unblemished lamb or goat. Life would be ensured by the blood of an innocent animal that was sacrificed. Much later, the blood of Christ would ensure the promise of eternal life for us all, an innocent man sacrificed for the sins of the world.

One source observes, "Inside their homes, the Israelites ate a meal of roast lamb, bitter herbs, and bread made without yeast. Unleavened bread could be made quickly because the dough did not have to rise. Thus, they could leave at any time. Bitter herbs signified the bitterness of slavery."⁴ Before the Israelites left Egypt, God was preparing them for victory even though it hadn't happened yet. Their preparation was an act of faith in the One true God of Israel.

In our own lives, there are times when it seems God is preparing us for a victory before we experience it for ourselves. In His faithfulness He brings all the working parts of our stories into alignment, and we witness His mighty hand in our lives only after He has prepared our hearts for the victory. In faith we can move forward knowing that God is the giver of the victory!

Read Exodus 12:31-42 in your Bible. How did Pharaoh and the Egyptians respond to the events of the first Passover?

What happened to the Israelites after the Passover?

Why was Pharaoh hesitant until this point to let the Israelites leave Egypt?

Based on this passage, how would you describe the character and action of God?

No matter how big the obstacles in your path may be, always remember your God is bigger and more powerful; and He is able to lead you in the trickiest and most chaotic of times. God is in control, and He will be a faithful companion as you fight for the dream that He has placed in your heart. No matter what "pharaohs" stand in your way, the Dream Giver will not leave you or forsake you. He will be with you every step of the way as you trust in Him.

GROUP SESSION GUIDE: WEEK 3

Fighting for the Dream

*As you fight for your dreams,
sometimes it gets worse before it gets better.
Our dreams require constant trust
in the Lord, but we can trust Him with our victory.*

Welcome/Prayer/Icebreaker (5–10 minutes)

Welcome to session 3 of *She Dreams*. This week we explored the ways in which opposition and haters can try to throw us off our plans; but when we trust in God's faithfulness and gather helpers along the way, we can stay focused on our dreams. Take a moment to open with prayer, and then go around the circle and name someone who has been a helper or supporter to you as you pursue your dreams—whether past or present.

Video (about 25 minutes)

Play the video segment for session 3, completing the following notes as you watch. Feel free to add notes about anything that resonates with you or that you want to be sure to remember.

—*Video Notes*—

Scriptures: Exodus 4:31*b*; 5:22; 6:1; 7:3-5

As you fight for the dream, sometimes it gets _____ before it gets _____.

_____ won't get you where you need to go.

Do not doubt God's _____ in our dreams.

Don't expect _____ in the middle of the journey. If and when you do see your dreams come true, those usually come at the _____.

Group Discussion (20–25 minutes for a 60-minute session; 30–35 minutes for a 90-minute session)

Video Discussion

- What excuses or fears keep you from moving toward your dreams?

Personal Lessons Review and Discussion

Day 1

1. Integrity and obedience matter as we pursue our God-sized dreams. The Lord sees us and knows us as we are. If He is partnering with us to chase after big dreams, we need to stand firm in who God has called us to be.
   - Why do integrity and obedience matter as we pursue our dreams?

2. As we pursue our God-sized dreams, there will be things that we need to take care of along the way. There will be things left undone that find us, haters and opposition who will come at us, and supporters or partners who need to be gathered. No matter what, we need to do what is in our power to do.
   - What next steps that are within your reach and power to do can you take toward seeing your dream become reality? (page 58)

Day 2

1. We can't control how people treat us, but we can choose how we treat those who oppose our dreams; and we can choose to stand our ground no matter how hard it may be. It's when haters come against our dreams or personhood that we are faced with the opportunity to either receive the offense or disrespect they're offering or stand our ground, even more convinced of what God is doing in and through us.

- Take turns reading Exodus 5. How did Pharaoh oppose Moses? (page 59)
- How do you think Moses and Aaron felt after their encounter with Pharaoh? (page 59)

2. Moses told the people of Israel what God planned to do; but under the weight of their slavery, they buckled. They didn't want to hear about Moses' big dreams anymore. Understandably, their discouragement kept them from believing the good plans Moses shared. Discouragement can have the same effect in us. But if we keep listening to God's voice, His voice will be louder than anyone who opposes our dreams.
    - Take turns reading Exodus 6:1-13 aloud. How did God encourage Moses after his encounter with Pharaoh? (page 61)
    - What are some ways we can listen closely to God and learn to hear His voice above any opposition or haters who come against us?

Day 3

1. As we chase our dreams, we need to remember to savor our days, right where we are, and trust God's timing. You may not be where you want to be, but you aren't where you used to be. The dream doesn't magically happen overnight. It happens with one good choice after another, one prayer after another, and one step after another.
    - Read Isaiah 55:8-9. How is this good news for a dreamer? (page 63)
    - What progress toward your dream have you already seen in your life? (page 63) Take a minute to name and celebrate together even baby steps toward your dreams.

Day 4

1. Moses had haters, no doubt about that; but he also had helpers. He had those who journeyed alongside him, believed in what God was doing within him, and stood with him when the going got incredibly tough. The same is true of us. We may encounter haters, but we also have helpers who journey alongside us one step at a time to see our dreams become reality.
    - Take turns reading Exodus 7:1-13. How would you describe the friendship between Moses and Aaron? How would you describe Aaron's role in the Exodus? (page 67)

- Read Ecclesiastes 4:9-12. Why is it necessary to have a helper as you chase your dreams? (page 68)

Day 5

1. Moses' God-given dream of freedom for Israel was bigger than the obstacles, oppressors, and even Egyptian gods that he encountered. He fought for the dream, and all of Egypt and Israel witnessed the mighty hand of God.
   - Review the ten plagues on pages 69-70. How were the plagues a display of both God's power and faithfulness and Pharaoh's opposition to Moses' dream?
   - What real or potential obstacles stand in the way of your dream becoming reality? (page 71) How might these obstacles become a display of God's power and faithfulness?

2. No matter how big the obstacles in your path may be, always remember your God is bigger and more powerful; and He is able to lead you in the trickiest and most chaotic of times. God is in control, and He will be a faithful companion as you fight for the dream that He has placed in your heart. No matter what "pharaohs" stand in your way, the Dream Giver will not leave you or forsake you.
   - Review your notes on Day 5 about the Passover (page 72). What was the purpose of the Passover? (page 72)
   - Take turns reading Exodus 12:31-42. Based on this passage, how would you describe the character and action of God? (page 73)
   - How does trusting in God's goodness help you persevere as you chase your dreams?

Becoming a Dreamer (10–15 minutes—90-minute session only)

Divide into groups of two to three for the following:

- If someone has discouraged you in your journey toward your dream, share how that has impacted you and the way you see your dream (see page 61). Rather than talking about the individual, stay focused on how the opposition has affected you. Then share the declaration you wrote (page 62) and encourage one another to press on toward your dreams.

Closing Prayer (5 minutes)

Close the session by sharing personal prayer requests and praying together. In addition to praying out loud for one another, ask for courage and bravery to stand firm against any opposition that might come against you and your God-sized dream. Give thanks for helpers along the way and for God's faithfulness every step of the journey.

Week 4

Don't Give Up on the Daydream

Moses Leads the Exodus
(Exodus 12:32–15:21)

When the going gets tough, God is still in control.
He is still the Dream Giver.

DAY 1: DUST YOURSELF OFF

As we begin week 4 of our study, I pray that you've been encouraged to know that your dreams matter and never deserve to be left on the shelf, collecting dust. The pursuit of your dreams invites you to live the life you were created for. Nothing less. You were created for a beautiful, wonderful, albeit sometimes messy life!

Read chapter 7 of the *She Dreams* book, "Dust Yourself Off," noting below any insights or encouragement you gain from your reading:

Today you read about one of my failed ventures, one I thought was a sure winner! It turned out to be an epic failure even though I thought my plan was foolproof. After I got over feeling sorry for myself, I had to get back up, dust myself off, and carry on. I wasn't a failure because things didn't go as planned. I was a learner, willing to try; and when things didn't work out, I chose to learn from my experience. I'm so thankful I did. I had much to learn, and my failed experience didn't leave me feeling like I was completely incapable of pursuing my dreams. In fact, it reminded me that life is full of ups and downs, but my choice to get back up, dust myself off, and keep going would serve me well because the dream doesn't usually come easy! You and I aren't made by the failures we have but by how we react to them. We have an enormous opportunity to grow through our trying times.

What lessons have you learned through past failed ventures or dreams?

How have those experiences affected how you pursue your dreams?

When I've felt like a failure, when everything I desire has seemed out of reach, I've found comfort in Psalm 40. The psalmist's confidence in God coupled with a cry for help perfectly echoes the state of my heart when it's time to get back up, dust myself off, and move forward toward the dreams God has for me. This psalm offers us encouragement for those times when things don't go as planned. Use Psalm 40:1-11 today as a springboard for prayer. If you want, write your prayer below.

DAY 2: LIVING A LIFE OF POWER

A few years ago, I sensed the Lord encouraging me to rely on His power rather than my own abilities. I could go on being continually surprised at the events in my life, or I could walk in the boldness and power of God and live the life He had for me. I could expect Him to hear me when I called. I could expect His power to be on display when I did as He asked. I could expect His love and faithfulness to always be with me. This was the invitation God offered to me. I didn't realize, like many of us, how much I had attributed the good things happening in my life to my own skills. He reminded me that He was behind it all along. He was the Giver of victory. The Giver of power. The Giver of boldness. He would both give and fulfill my dreams.

No matter what obstacles we encounter, we can trust in the Dream Giver, the One who loves us, calls us, and offers us His power. We don't have to rely on our strengths, insecurities, or doubts to lead us. God will and God can.

Describe a time when you had to choose between relying on yourself or relying on the power and faithfulness of God:

Today we're digging into one of the most iconic passages of the Old Testament: the Israelites' escape from Egypt. Exodus 13 and 14 detail exactly how the Israelites, after four hundred years of slavery, found freedom despite Pharaoh's last-ditch effort to stop his free labor from making their grand exit.

Read Exodus 13:17–14:4 in your Bible. What evidence of God's wisdom and power do you find in these verses?

How would you describe the character of God based on this passage?

God knew what He was doing when He led the Israelites along the longer path to the Promised Land. He knew the limits of what they could handle and their ingrained reliance on the power and providence of Pharaoh. In His foresight, He led them to a place where their Egyptian oppressors would assume they could catch them, but actually the Egyptians would witness the power of the Lord.

Read Exodus 14:5-14 in your Bible. What words or phrases from these verses convey the insecurity of the Israelites?

I can't imagine the fear the Israelites felt as they saw the Egyptian troops racing after them while they walked on foot. Tens of thousands of families, with little ones to senior citizens among them, saw their oppressors chase them in chariots. To the Egyptians, the Israelites were sitting ducks to be devoured. Even though it appeared they were surrounded by their enemy, their Emancipator was present and ready to fight their battles.

Has there been a time in your life when it felt as though what sought to oppress you would conquer you? If so, describe it briefly:

> We spend most of our lives avoiding desperate moments. We don't want for a second to be in a place where we desperately need God to show up, but the truth is He is still the God of miracles. Our God is one who shows up when our life is a mess—when change, however magic or tragic, smacks us upside the head. He is ready to lead us through the unthinkable. To Moses on the edge of the Red Sea, He said, "Why are you crying out to me? Tell the people to get moving!" (Exodus 14:15). God was not absent when Moses

> and the Israelite nation needed Him most. He was ready, unshaken by the situation.
>
> —*She Dreams*, pages 123-124

By the power of God, we can refuse to be afraid. We can stand still and watch the Lord rescue us. The Lord Himself will fight for us. We can stay calm. His power is greater than ours. His strength is unmatched. He has no rival. No equal. He will display His power, and we can trust Him. We can trust Him with every inch of our lives and every ounce of our battle.

Read Exodus 14:15-31 in your Bible. In what ways do we see the glory and power of God on display here?

Why do you think God told Moses to raise his staff?

Describe the Israelites' behavior before and after God parted the Red Sea.

Before:

After:

God had plans to rescue the Israelites whether they were in fear at the edge of the Red Sea or whether they were confident that God would save them although their enemy was in sight. Our God will not be stopped. Just as God ordained freedom for the Israelites, God will not be stopped in bringing freedom for us. We can walk in the power of God, as Moses did, with confidence that He will lead. He is an on-time God and will reveal His glory and power when we least expect it and when we need it most. To God be the glory!

DAY 3: GET YOUR HEAD OUT OF THE SAND

Read chapter 8 of the *She Dreams* book, "Get Your Head Out of the Sand," noting below any insights or encouragement you gain from your reading:

What are some of your strengths and weakneses? List them below:

Strengths   Weaknesses

How have your strengths contributed to the pursuit of your dreams?

How have your weaknesses slowed your progress toward your dreams?

Each of us has strengths or gifts, and each of us has weaknesses. Self-awareness is the first step to understanding how our strengths and weaknesses affect our trajectory toward our dreams, and we can seek wisdom to help us. Wisdom will guide us when our weaknesses threaten to derail our progress.

As you read in chapter 8, wisdom—when sought and embraced—is a valuable tool on our journey to our God-sized dreams. We won't ever regret our search for wisdom. Without it, it may take us much longer than we anticipated and more tears than necessary to be who we want to be and get to where we want to go. There is no use trying to be awesome at everything, because, dear friend, we weren't built like that. We were built with strengths that can be maximized and a heart that can grow, stretch, and learn.

As we become aware of our weaknesses, we can celebrate the truth that God is still willing to partner with us, no matter how much weight our weaknesses carry in our lives. When our weaknesses get the better of us and set us back, God will draw near; and we will be able to move forward with confidence that the Dream Giver won't forsake us simply because we are weak in certain areas of our life.

Offer a prayer, asking for wisdom as you pursue your dreams. If you want, write your prayer below.

Extra Insight

Proverbs 2:1-11 describes the benefits of pursuing wisdom.

DAY 4: PRAISE THE DREAM GIVER

The year 2013 was one of the hardest, sweetest, and most stretching years of my entire life. After court appointments, a hefty amount of paperwork, immigration interviews, and medical exams, I wept uncontrollably in front of a full courtroom of friends and family as my son's adoption was finalized. On that day in that courtroom with that judge, what heaven had spoken to me years before was fulfilled on the earth. I stood in awe at the glory and power of God to fulfill the dreams He had placed within the deepest parts of my heart. With my son on my hip and my husband by my side, I praised the Lord who calls us to wild dreams. I praised the God who gives us wisdom, hope, peace, and strength to carry on when it feels like the journey is too difficult and the terrain too rocky. I praised the Dream Giver.

As we pursue our dreams, we will experience both small and big victories; and in those moments we must stop everything, throw up our hands, and praise the One who calls us, delivers us, defends us, and gives us the victory! The God of Abraham, Isaac, Jacob, Joseph, and Moses is the same God who leads us to pursue our dreams. May we give Him all the glory!

What victories, big or small, has God given you so far as you pursue your dreams?

What did you learn about His character in the process?

As we praise the Dream Giver for all He has done for us, it stretches our belief in who He is, what He can do, and what He will do on our behalf. The act of praise rightly places God—rather than our own fear, doubt, or abilities—on the throne of our lives. In praise, we acknowledge that we serve the God of the impossible, the God who sees and delivers. The Apostle Paul stated it perfectly in Romans when he said:

> [1]*And so, dear brothers and sisters, I plead with you to give your bodies to God because of all he has done for you. Let them be a living and holy sacrifice—the kind he will find acceptable. This is truly the way to worship him.* [2]*Don't copy the behavior and customs of this world, but let God transform you into a new person by changing the way you think. Then you will learn to know God's will for you, which is good and pleasing and perfect.*
>
> (Romans 12:1-2)

After the Israelites finally left Egypt and Moses led them through the parted Red Sea, they arrived safely on the other shore—every single one of them. Pharaoh's army, which had pursued them in chariots, was swallowed up by the sea. Seconds before God had parted the Red Sea, the Israelites had groaned, asking why Moses had brought them out of Egypt only to be pursued by Pharaoh and die. Yet God in His sovereignty did the miraculous work of providing a way through the waters. Freedom for Israel was a promise He planned to keep! "When the people of Israel saw the mighty power that the Lord had unleashed against the Egyptians, they were filled with awe before him. They put their faith in the Lord and in his servant Moses" (Exodus 14:31).

Read Exodus 15:1-21 below, and underline the descriptions of the miracles God performed on behalf of the Israelites:

¹**Then Moses and the people of Israel sang this song to the Lord:**

"I will sing to the Lord,
    for he has triumphed gloriously;
he has hurled both horse and rider
    into the sea.
²The Lord is my strength and my song;
    he has given me victory.
This is my God, and I will praise him—
    my father's God, and I will exalt him!
³The Lord is a warrior;
    Yahweh is his name!
⁴Pharaoh's chariots and army
    he has hurled into the sea.
The finest of Pharaoh's officers
    are drowned in the Red Sea.
⁵The deep waters gushed over them;
    they sank to the bottom like a stone.

⁶"Your right hand, O Lord,
    is glorious in power.
Your right hand, O Lord,
    smashes the enemy.
⁷In the greatness of your majesty,
    you overthrow those who rise against you.
You unleash your blazing fury;
    it consumes them like straw.
⁸At the blast of your breath,
    the waters piled up!

Extra Insight

One commentary notes that the mention of the "Red Sea" [in Exodus 13:18] is actually 'Reed Sea,' an apparent reference to the shallow waters at the northern end of the Gulf of Suez.... It is not necessary, to be faithful to the biblical account, to believe that the water of the Reed Sea was hundreds of feet deep, as it would be in the Red Sea proper...or even in the southern end of the Gulf of Suez. Water ten feet deep would be just as effective a barrier."[1]

The surging waters stood straight like a wall;
> in the heart of the sea the deep waters became hard.

⁹"The enemy boasted, 'I will chase them
> and catch up with them.
I will plunder them
> and consume them.
I will flash my sword;
> my powerful hand will destroy them.'
¹⁰But you blew with your breath,
> and the sea covered them.
They sank like lead
> in the mighty waters.

¹¹"Who is like you among the gods, O Lord—
> glorious in holiness,
awesome in splendor,
> performing great wonders?
¹²You raised your right hand,
> and the earth swallowed our enemies.

¹³"With your unfailing love you lead
> the people you have redeemed.
In your might, you guide them
> to your sacred home.
¹⁴The peoples hear and tremble;
> anguish grips those who live in Philistia.
¹⁵The leaders of Edom are terrified;
> the nobles of Moab tremble.
All who live in Canaan melt away;
> ¹⁶terror and dread fall upon them.
The power of your arm
> makes them lifeless as stone
until your people pass by, O Lord,
> until the people you purchased pass by.
¹⁷You will bring them in and plant them on your own mountain—
> the place, O Lord, reserved for your own dwelling,
> the sanctuary, O Lord, that your hands have established.
> ¹⁸The Lord will reign forever and ever!"

¹⁹When Pharaoh's horses, chariots, and charioteers rushed into the sea, the Lord brought the water crashing down on them. But the people of Israel had walked through the middle of the sea on dry ground!

²⁰Then Miriam the prophet, Aaron's sister, took a tambourine and led all the women as they played their tambourines and danced. ²¹And Miriam sang this song:

> **"Sing to the Lord,**
> **for he has triumphed gloriously;**
> **he has hurled both horse and rider**
> **into the sea."**

Based on these verses, what did the Israelites believe about their God after witnessing these miraculous events?

This exquisite poetry and prose was praise offered by the Israelites to God for all He had done for them. They were in awe at the splendor and power of God to act on their behalf. In their own words, they detailed exactly how God had saved them from destruction and annihilation even though they had questioned Moses before God parted the sea.

As we've discussed, the Israelites had been enslaved in Egypt for over four hundred years and were accustomed to the cultural and religious customs of Egypt. They had some understanding of God's power as they witnessed the ten plagues, yet their complaints to Moses before God parted the Red Sea are evidence that they still doubted God's care for them. Prior to the last verse of Exodus 14, the Israelites grumbled and complained while Moses fought for the dream of freedom; but they changed their tune when they witnessed the walls of water created for their escape, responding with a song of praise for their Deliverer.

Reread the Israelites' song of praise again, one section at a time, summarizing the theme of each set of verses below in your own words:

Verses 1-3:

Verses 4-10:

Verses 11-19:

One commentator offers this helpful explanation for Miriam's song:

> The great burden of the first three verses is personal. The first person pronoun occurs eight times. God, who has been abstract and impersonal, has acted personally for them. The Maker of the universe is indeed their personal God....
>
> The second stanza of the song (15:4-10) emphasizes the contrast between the might of the Egyptians and the might of God. The second person pronoun is prominent; God is the dominant reality. As he promised, they now know him to be Lord. The boast of earth's mighty is nothing in contrast with the mere breath of God's nostrils (vv. 8-10).
>
> The third stanza (vv. 11-19) contrasts God and the gods. As God's unique character has been shown through delivering his people, so it will be seen in his triumph over the nations (Philistia, Edom, Moab, and Canaan) as he leads the Israelites into their inheritance. Here we see the fulfillment of 8:10 and similar statements: there is none like God.[2]

The Israelites' song of praise to God is a reminder that we can praise God for the specific actions He has taken in our own lives. He is a great and mighty God, worthy of our praise! We might not understand how every single detail of our lives will work out, but we can praise the Dream Giver for all He has done.

At the beginning of today's study, I shared about the praise I offered God after my son's adoption was finalized; but before the dream became reality, when we experienced only small victories toward the overall goal of adoption, we also praised the Dream Giver. For each victory, whether it was a clean bill of health for my son or an immigration meeting that leaned in our favor, I couldn't help giving God the glory for His tender care.

Our God is in the details, working on our behalf for our good. May we give Him all the praise!

In the space below, write a short song of praise for God's action and care on your behalf:

DAY 5: BY FAITH

As our week comes to a close, we'll spend time today reflecting on the One true God—the God of the Israelites who makes Himself available to all who call on His name; to those who dream; to those who, by faith, partner with Him for greater things. We've discovered that the dreams we have in our hearts don't grow on accident, and they aren't to be ignored. They are a part of us; and if we pursue them, our lives will never be the same. What we value, what we fight for, and who we become are all part of the glorious process of pursuing a dream.

This week we've seen that Moses, the dreamer who chose to live the life He was created for, faced some uphill battles: the plagues, the death of Egypt's firstborn, the great chase across the desert. You know, stuff legends are made of! We may be tempted to assume that Moses is almost superhuman due to the events of his life. It's understandable. Who is born in the midst of genocide and goes undetected by the powers that be? Who is adopted by Pharaoh's daughter and lives the life of a royal, immersed in the culture and able to enjoy every privilege possible? Who murders a man, escapes punishment, and starts a new life? Who stands before a burning bush and has a chat with God? Who raises his staff and plagues hit Egypt? Who leads over a million people through the Red Sea? Moses, that's who. But don't mistake him for a superhero; he was a man who partnered with God for the dream of freedom.

Moses, like you and me, was born on purpose for a purpose and given gifts, skills, and abilities. Moses, like you and me, had good days and days of defeat. Moses, like you and me, was beloved by God and invited to partner with Him for dreams that exceeded Moses' wildest dreams.

How has your faith in God influenced the steps you've taken to see your dream come true?

Read Hebrews 11 on the following pages and circle every instance of the phrase "by faith" (or a similar variation):

¹*Faith shows the reality of what we hope for; it is the evidence of things we cannot see.* ²*Through their faith, the people in days of old earned a good reputation.*

³*By faith we understand that the entire universe was formed at God's command, that what we now see did not come from anything that can be seen.*

⁴*It was by faith that Abel brought a more acceptable offering to God than Cain did. Abel's offering gave evidence that he was a righteous man, and God showed his approval of his gifts. Although Abel is long dead, he still speaks to us by his example of faith.*

⁵*It was by faith that Enoch was taken up to heaven without dying—"he disappeared, because God took him." For before he was taken up, he was known as a person who pleased God.* ⁶*And it is impossible to please God without faith. Anyone who wants to come to him must believe that God exists and that he rewards those who sincerely seek him.*

⁷*It was by faith that Noah built a large boat to save his family from the flood. He obeyed God, who warned him about things that had never happened before. By his faith Noah condemned the rest of the world, and he received the righteousness that comes by faith.*

⁸It was by faith that Abraham obeyed when God called him to leave home and go to another land that God would give him as his inheritance. He went without knowing where he was going. ⁹And even when he reached the land God promised him, he lived there by faith— for he was like a foreigner, living in tents. And so did Isaac and Jacob, who inherited the same promise. ¹⁰Abraham was confidently looking forward to a city with eternal foundations, a city designed and built by God.

¹¹It was by faith that even Sarah was able to have a child, though she was barren and was too old. She believed that God would keep his promise. ¹²And so a whole nation came from this one man who was as good as dead—a nation with so many people that, like the stars in the sky and the sand on the seashore, there is no way to count them.

¹³All these people died still believing what God had promised them. They did not receive what was promised, but they saw it all from a distance and welcomed it. They agreed that they were foreigners and nomads here on earth. ¹⁴Obviously people who say such things are looking forward to a country they can call their own. ¹⁵If they had longed for the country they came from, they could have gone back. ¹⁶But they were looking for a better place, a heavenly homeland. That is why God is not ashamed to be called their God, for he has prepared a city for them.

¹⁷It was by faith that Abraham offered Isaac as a sacrifice when God was testing him. Abraham, who had received God's promises, was ready to sacrifice his only son, Isaac, even though God had told him, "Isaac is the son through whom your descendants will be counted." ¹⁹Abraham reasoned that if Isaac died, God was able to bring him back to life again. And in a sense, Abraham did receive his son back from the dead.

²⁰It was by faith that Isaac promised blessings for the future to his sons, Jacob and Esau.

Don't Give Up on the Daydream

²¹It was by faith that Jacob, when he was old and dying, blessed each of Joseph's sons and bowed in worship as he leaned on his staff.

²²It was by faith that Joseph, when he was about to die, said confidently that the people of Israel would leave Egypt. He even commanded them to take his bones with them when they left.

²³It was by faith that Moses' parents hid him for three months when he was born. They saw that God had given them an unusual child, and they were not afraid to disobey the king's command.

²⁴It was by faith that Moses, when he grew up, refused to be called the son of Pharaoh's daughter. ²⁵He chose to share the oppression of God's people instead of enjoying the fleeting pleasures of sin. ²⁶He thought it was better to suffer for the sake of Christ than to own the treasures of Egypt, for he was looking ahead to his great reward. ²⁷It was by faith that Moses left the land of Egypt, not fearing the king's anger. He kept right on going because he kept his eyes on the one who is invisible. ²⁸It was by faith that Moses commanded the people of Israel to keep the Passover and to sprinkle blood on the doorposts so that the angel of death would not kill their firstborn sons.

²⁹It was by faith that the people of Israel went right through the Red Sea as though they were on dry ground. But when the Egyptians tried to follow, they were all drowned.

³⁰It was by faith that the people of Israel marched around Jericho for seven days, and the walls came crashing down.

³¹It was by faith that Rahab the prostitute was not destroyed with the people in her city who refused to obey God. For she had given a friendly welcome to the spies.

³²How much more do I need to say? It would take too long to recount the stories of the faith of Gideon, Barak, Samson, Jephthah, David, Samuel, and all the prophets. ³³By faith these people overthrew kingdoms, ruled with justice, and received what God had promised them. They shut the

mouths of lions, ³⁴quenched the flames of fire, and escaped death by the edge of the sword. Their weakness was turned to strength. They became strong in battle and put whole armies to flight. ³⁵Women received their loved ones back again from death.

But others were tortured, refusing to turn from God in order to be set free. They placed their hope in a better life after the resurrection. ³⁶Some were jeered at, and their backs were cut open with whips. Others were chained in prisons. ³⁷Some died by stoning, some were sawed in half, and others were killed with the sword. Some went about wearing skins of sheep and goats, destitute and oppressed and mistreated. ³⁸They were too good for this world, wandering over deserts and mountains, hiding in caves and holes in the ground.

³⁹All these people earned a good reputation because of their faith, yet none of them received all that God had promised. ⁴⁰For God had something better in mind for us, so that they would not reach perfection without us.

What is significant about the repetition of this phrase?

How would you summarize Hebrews 11 in your own words?

What role does faith play as you pursue your dreams?

It was by faith that the saints of the Scriptures pursued their extraordinary dreams. Some "overthrew kingdoms, ruled with justice, and received what God had promised them. They shut the mouths of lions, quenched the flames of fire, and escaped death by the edge of the sword. Their weakness was turned to strength" (Hebrews 11:33-34). While some tasted victory, others, by faith, experienced torture and imprisonment. Even though the events of their lives varied, as ours do, their faith was the thread that set them apart. They chose faith as the foundation of their dreams, hopes, and desires.

In our own lives, by faith we can step out, step up, and pursue the dreams God has for us. By faith, we can live the life we were created for—nothing less. By faith, we can partner with the Dream Giver for the impossible; and even though things may not always work out as we planned, we can remember that we are pursuing a heavenly reward: life eternal with the Dream Giver. Hallelujah!

Write your own "by faith" statement as it pertains to your dreams:

GROUP SESSION GUIDE: WEEK 4

Don't Give Up on the Daydream

As we pursue our dreams, we have to be vulnerable, fierce, and focused. We can be sure that God is in control, even when the going gets tough!

Welcome/Prayer/Icebreaker (5–10 minutes)

Welcome to session 4 of *She Dreams*. I hope you are beginning to see that the pursuit of your dreams invites you to live the life you were created for. Nothing less. You were created for a beautiful, wonderful, albeit sometimes messy life! Take a moment to open with prayer, and then go around the circle and briefly describe a past failed venture or experience—a time when things didn't turn out as you planned.

Video (about 25 minutes)

Play the video segment for session 4, completing the following notes as you watch. Feel free to add notes about anything that resonates with you or that you want to be sure to remember.

—Video Notes—

Scriptures: *Exodus* 12:40-42; 13:17, 20-22; 14:1-4, 11-12, 13; *1 Corinthians* 10:1-4

The dream demands the dreamer is vulnerable, _____, and _____.

We have to _____ our vulnerability.

We have to keep our _____ on the Dream Giver.

Don't Give Up on the Daydream

We have to believe we are _____ of the dream.

Group Discussion (20–25 minutes for a 60-minute session; 30–35 minutes for a 90-minute session)

Video Discussion

- What makes your dream seem out of reach? Are there challenges or thoughts that make you want to throw in the towel?

Personal Lessons Review and Discussion

Day 1

1. Life is full of ups and downs, but choosing to get back up, dust ourselves off, and keep going will serve us well because dreams don't usually come easy! You and I aren't made by the failures we have but by how we react to them. We have an enormous opportunity to grow through our trying times.
   - Recall the failed venture or experience you shared at the beginning of the session. What lessons have you learned through this and other past failed ventures or dreams? (page 82)
   - How have those experiences affected how you pursue your dreams? (page 82)

Day 2

1. God knew what He was doing when He led the Israelites along the longer path to the Promised Land. He knew the limits of what they could handle and their ingrained reliance on the power and providence of Pharaoh. In His foresight, He led them to a place where their Egyptian oppressors would assume they could catch them, but actually the Egyptians would witness the power of the Lord.
   - Take turns reading Exodus 13:17–14:4. What evidence of God's power do you find in these verses? (page 83)
   - How would you describe the character of God based on this passage? (page 83)

2. By the power of God, we can refuse to be afraid. We can stand still and watch the Lord rescue us. The Lord Himself will fight for us. We can stay

100   She Dreams

calm. His power is greater than ours. His strength is unmatched. He has no rival. No equal. He will display His power, and we can trust Him. We can trust Him with every inch of our lives and every ounce of our battle.
- Take turns reading Exodus 14:15-31 aloud. In what ways is God's glory and power on display here? Describe the Israelites' behavior before and after God parted the Red Sea. (page 85)
- Do you find it easy or difficult to trust in God's timing, strength, and character when you face your battles? Why do you think that is?

Day 3

1. Wisdom—when sought and embraced—is a valuable tool on our journey to our God-sized dreams. Without it, it may take us much longer than we anticipated and more tears than necessary to be who we want to be and get to where we want to go. There is no use trying to be awesome at everything, we weren't built like that. We were built with strengths that can be maximized and a heart that can grow, stretch, and learn.
    - Have you ever found yourself attempting to be awesome at everything? Describe that experience. What did you discover about your strengths and weaknesses?
    - Take turns reading Proverbs 2:1-11. Why do you think wisdom is essential when our weaknesses threaten to derail our progress?

Day 4

1. As we praise the Dream Giver for all He has done for us, it stretches our belief in who He is, what He can do, and what He will do on our behalf. The act of praise rightly places God—rather than our own fear, doubt, or abilities—on the throne of our lives.
    - How does praising God for all he has done stretch our beliefs in who He is and what He can do?
    - What do you want to praise God for right now as you think about all He has done for you in your pursuit of your dream?

2. We might not understand how every single detail of our lives will work out, but we can praise the Dream Giver for all He has done. Our God is in the details, working on our behalf for our good.

- Take turns reading Exodus 15:1-22. How does this song of praise show us how God is in every detail working for our victory?
- What did the Israelites believe after witnessing the miraculous events listed in this passage? (page 91)

Day 5
1. The dreams we have in our hearts don't grow on accident, and they aren't to be ignored. They are a part of us; and if we pursue them, our lives will never be the same. What we value, what we fight for, and who we become are all part of the glorious process of being a dreamer.
    - Where do you believe God is in the life of your dream? (page 94)

2. It was by faith that the saints of the Scriptures pursued their extraordinary dreams. Some overthrew kingdoms, ruled with justice, and received what God had promised them. They shut the mouths of lions, quenched the flames of fire, and escaped death by the edge of the sword. Their weakness was turned to strength. In our own lives, by faith we can step out, step up, and pursue the dreams God has for us. By faith, we can live the life we were created for—nothing less.
    - Refer to your notes on Hebrews 11 on page 97. How would you summarize this passage? (page 97)
    - What role does faith play in pursuing your dreams? (page 97)

Becoming a Dreamer (10–15 minutes—90-minute session only)

Divide into groups of two to three for the following:

- Share your faith statements from Day 5 on page 98. How might declaring your faith in God to do more than you could ever ask or imagine give you extra focus and fierceness as you go after your dream?

Closing Prayer (5 minutes)

Close the session by sharing personal prayer requests and praying together. In addition to praying out loud for one another, ask God to give you faith to believe that he is good and faithful, strong, and always, always, always on time.

Week 5

Growing Pains

Moses in the Wilderness
(Exodus 15:22–19:6)

Pursuing our dreams provides ample opportunity for spiritual growth.

DAY 1: COMPARISON IS THE THIEF OF DREAMS

Read chapter 9 of the *She Dreams* book, "Stop Scrolling and Start Rolling," noting below any insights or encouragement you gain from your reading:

In chapter 9, you read about the dangers of comparing yourself to others. Comparison isn't a new demon to fight but one most of us have struggled with for as long as we can remember. Yet its devastating effects are never to be underestimated. When we compare our life to another's, whether in person or on screen, we can easily dismiss what the Lord is building within us. We do ourselves a great disservice when we compare the shiny highlights of another's life with the hard parts of our own. Who we are, what God is doing within us, and the person we are becoming are unique, one-of-a-kind, and incredibly special. Rather than compare our looks, accomplishments, platform, or possessions, we can accept our story and live in the fullness of God.

Do you struggle with comparing your life to others around you or online? If so, describe your struggle briefly:

More often than not, we don't fully understand the complications or hardships of the very person we are comparing ourselves to. God equips us to fight our battles, but He doesn't equip us to live someone else's life. Paul instructs us in Ephesians to "lead a life worthy of your calling, for you have been called by God" (Ephesians 4:1). We are each called by God to partner with Him as we pursue our dreams. The dreams or accomplishments of another never diminish the beauty and wonder of our own dreams and accomplishments. God longs to lead each of us to a life of humility and gentleness in every season, rather than leaving us feeling like a failure because we don't have "her" (you know who she is) life.

I have a threenager—you know, the three-year-old going on thirteen—and a strong-willed seven-year-old. My threenager has big feelings and impressive lung capacity, and he can wear his mama out! At my wits' end, with too much coffee in my belly and tired eyes, I find myself comparing my season of life with little ones to those whose kids are in school full-time. I compare the chaos of my weekdays—which include work, a busy three-year-old who begs (at the top of his lungs) for yogurt at the grocery store, and all that I try to stuff into my days—to the brunching mamas who go to spin class five days a week. I salivate over their weekdays like a dog with rabies, and then I remember no one wins when I compare my season or situation to those brunching mommies. My season is mine for a reason. The Lord has something for me to learn. Something for me to do. He has something precious for me that is only accessible in this season of life.

Have you ever felt convinced that someone else's life or season is dreamy compared to yours? Chances are you have. In those moments, whisper to yourself, "Who I am is enough, and these are precious days. God is with me, and there is beauty in my season."

In your own words, write a mantra you can repeat to yourself when you feel the temptation to compare yourself to someone else's life or season:

> Never forget, dear friend, you are a beautiful woman. You are handcrafted, gifted, and unique. If you haven't heard that today, I'm happy to drop that bomb in your lap. . . .
>
> There is room for all of us at the table. There is room for your gifts, your story, your ideas, and your dreams. There is also room for her gifts, her story, her ideas, and her dreams. Rather than demonize another's past, present, appearance, or track record, we can celebrate one another.
>
> —*She Dreams*, pages 151-152

DAY 2: PROVISION FOR THE VISION

When my kids, who are regularly fed nutritious food, act as though they haven't eaten in days, I shake my head, because this mama cannot believe these ducklings would act like they are starving. No way, babies! You won't win this one! Except they do. Just last week we attended a backyard barbeque complete with all the fixin's you can imagine, not to mention the ice cream and cupcakes for dessert. After the barbeque came to a close, I strapped my kids in the car for the trek home. I assumed they might even fall asleep since they had full bellies and plenty of time in the sun. How wrong I was. Those little duckies begged for their daddy and me to stop for a full meal on the way home. We gave in to protein packs from the world's most popular coffee shop, and then and only then were they satisfied. I tell you now, not fifteen minutes after my son devoured that protein pack he asked what we were having for dinner. Bless.

You and I can be like children after a summer barbeque, with the needs of our belly met, and we wonder when, where, or how we'll be sustained again. Our patience is tested. We want what we want when we want it; and when can't have it when we want it, then we are mad!

Has there been a time in your life that you were angry or frustrated because you didn't know how the next phase would play out?

What did you learn from that experience?

The Israelites knew a thing or two about testing. After their triumphant crossing of the Red Sea, they were led into the wilderness. They now had life before the Red Sea and life after the Red Sea. As they passed between the walls of water, they experienced a birth of sorts. Like a newborn they cried and whined for the comforts of familiar territory, but it was no longer time for them to be in Egypt; their time, their birth, had come, and they could not go back. Everything would be different, and they, like a newborn, were completely dependent on their Caregiver.

Read these passages in your Bible, noting below *what* and *how* God provided for the Israelites:

Exodus 15:22-27

Exodus 16

How did some of the people disobey God's instructions regarding the manna, and what happened when they did?

God had a good plan for the Israelites that would test them and build them into the nation He desired them to be, but now they had to trust God for their every need instead of rely on their oppressors for food and housing. Although they were out of Egypt, Egypt wasn't out of them! They wanted the easy way, but God had no intention of offering them ease but rather opportunity to trust Him. By their complaints we can gather that the Israelites weren't raving fans of their new conditions—regardless of the fact that they had recently witnessed the power of God splitting a sea. Yet God was present in the wilderness, available and willing to meet their needs. He longed for their obedience and trust, which were necessary to develop a healthy relationship between the Creator and the created.

Reread Exodus 16:10, and summarize the significance of this verse:

In all of the Book of Exodus, this verse is one of my absolute favorites because the glory of the Lord in the cloud reminds me that God called the Israelites into the wilderness for their good, not their destruction. In the wilderness, God could prove Himself faithful without any distractions. He could become their Provider when they had no one else to rely on.

In our own lives, we often despise wilderness seasons, but God goes before us, leading the way for our good.

Read Jesus' words in John 6:48-51 in the margin. What did Jesus call Himself? How does He satisfy our spiritual needs—now and forever?

⁴⁸Yes, I am the bread of life! ⁴⁹Your ancestors ate manna in the wilderness, but they all died. ⁵⁰Anyone who eats the bread from heaven, however, will never die. ⁵¹I am the living bread that came down from heaven. Anyone who eats this bread will live forever; and this bread, which I will offer so the world may live, is my flesh."
(John 6:48-51)

The manna from heaven in the Old Testament and Jesus as the bread of life in the New Testament point to a God who longs to provide for us and sustain us. Like the gift of the Sabbath, it is a gift to rest and reflect on the One who is for us, leading us through the wilderness moments in order to see our dreams become reality. Praise Him!

Offer a prayer of gratitude for the provision the Dream Giver provides for the vision of your dreams. (If you want, write your prayer in the margin.)

DAY 3: USE WHAT'S IN YOUR HAND

Years ago I made a friend through a camp that serves families with a disabled family member. Since my oldest brother is disabled, my parents packed

Growing Pains 109

us up every year to make the trek down to sunny Santa Cruz, California, for family camp. The camp was founded by a strong woman named Joni Eareckson Tada, who lost all mobility from the neck down due to a diving accident in her teen years. Her life changed forever in that moment. Everything she expected her life to look like was gone in an instant. In her new normal she discovered she could paint marvelous works of art if she held the end of the paintbrush in her mouth. She painted pictures of still life, animals, and even people. Years after her diving accident, my parents were blessed by her testimony and fascinated with her paintings. Prints of her work proudly hung on the walls of my parents' home. They served as a constant reminder that you can use what's in your proverbial hand to pursue the dreams God placed within you.

Authors tap away on their keyboard, singers clutch a microphone, and painters wield their brush to create the masterpieces only they can create. As we dream, we can use what's in our hand to move forward in our journey to see our dreams come to pass. We can't sit by and hope everything happens on its own; we must engage our skills and abilities as we trust the Lord. We must roll up our sleeves and participate!

What is in your "hand" that you can use as you partner with God for your dreams?

Most days I grip a slim laptop in one hand and my purse in the other as I duck into my favorite coffee shop. I order my usual whole milk cappuccino before I plop down at a marble-top table for one. I snap on noise-canceling headphones and open my laptop to smack the keys on my keyboard. For me, my keyboard is what's in my hand to see my dreams come to pass as I partner with God.

Moses knew a thing or two about trusting the Lord and using what was in his hand to move forward in the dream God had given him. Earlier in Exodus, God allowed Moses' staff to turn into a snake. His staff represented the power of God, and it remained firmly in his hand as the plagues hit Egypt and the Israelites left Egypt by way of the Red Sea. Then in Exodus 17, we see God partnering with Moses to use what is in his hand for the providence and protection of Israel.

Read Exodus 17:1-7 in your Bible and answer the following questions.

How do you think Moses felt as the Israelites chided him?

What was Moses to do with his staff?

Moses was up to his ears with complaints as the Israelites criticized him for their lack of drinking water. (If you've ever felt tormented by thirst with no way to satisfy your desire, then you might understand the complaints of the people.) Without water, they knew they were in trouble. Although God had provided water at Marah, they were worried, once again, that God would not provide for them. God, in His providence, partnered with Moses to supply clean drinking water to the Israelites by way of his staff. In their lack and thirst, God made a way to provide in the wilderness.

Read 1 Corinthians 10:1-4 in the margin. According to the Apostle Paul, whom did the rock that was struck represent?

When the rock that represented Jesus was struck, what did everyone have access to?

The good news of the gospel is this: Jesus was struck, afflicted, and crucified; and because of His sacrifice, living water flowed out for all to receive—living

---

Extra Insight:

"Rephidim means *rests*, or *resting-places*, and is an appropriate name for the central part of the Wady Feiran—the most fertile spot in the whole peninsula [of Sinai], where there is usually abundant water, rich vegetation, and numerous palm-trees."[1]

¹I don't want you to forget, dear brothers and sisters, about our ancestors in the wilderness long ago. All of them were guided by a cloud that moved ahead of them, and all of them walked through the sea on dry ground. ²In the cloud and in the sea, all of them were baptized as followers of Moses. ³All of them ate the same spiritual food, ⁴and all of them drank the same spiritual water. For they drank from the spiritual rock that traveled with them, and that rock was Christ.
(1 Corinthians 10:1-4)

Growing Pains 111

water that would satisfy our souls. In Moses striking the rock, we are given a snippet of the Rock who would be struck for our freedom and redemption. Because of Jesus, we no longer would be cursed by the law but would have access to living water that will never run dry.

Yet in Exodus 17 we see that rather than cry out to God for water, the Israelites complain to Moses for their troubles. Even though they have witnessed God providing for them in times past, they argue and test rather than petition and pray for God's miraculous hand to provide for them.

It isn't just the Israelites who argue and test God; we do it too. Instead of praying to the God that we know beyond a shadow of a doubt can supply all of our needs, we complain and argue. We wonder if He brought us through one season only to abandon us in the next.

Have you ever caught yourself complaining and arguing rather than taking the matter to the Lord in prayer? If so, describe it briefly.

In our low moments, the ones when we feel tormented, we can call out to God, listen to His instructions, and partner with Him to grow through our troubles. Complaining and arguing will never lead us to a place of greater trust and partnership with God. We can heed the words written to the Philippians, "Don't worry about anything; instead, pray about everything. Tell God what you need, and thank him for all he has done" (Philippians 4:6). We may be surprised at His instructions. He may direct us to use what's in our hands—whether they be hands that bake, hands that hold babies, or hands that can be lifted in praise—to grow through our troubles and move forward toward the dreams in our hearts.

Write a prayer offering to use what's in your proverbial or literal hands to partner with God for your dreams:

Read Exodus 17:8-16 in your Bible. What do you notice about the name of Moses' staff?

Look back at Exodus 17:5. Whose staff is mentioned there?

In Exodus 17:9 we see that Moses refers to the staff as "the staff of God," and God refers to it in Exodus 17:5 as "your staff." Moses understood that the staff was provided by God and represented God's power. God entrusted the staff to Moses as a tool to reach the dream He had placed within Moses' heart. With the staff, God not only provided for the Israelites water from the rock at Rephidim but He also protected them against attackers when Moses raised his staff at the top of the hill. The Israelites were given victory over the Amalekites because the Lord saw fit to give it to them, but that victory involved the use of their gifts and skills. Moses was instructed to hold up the staff while Joshua led men into battle. It was a "both/and" situation.

Like the Israelites, we can enter into partnership with God for a "both/and" journey toward our dreams. And we can trust God for the victory as we engage in using what's in our hands: the gifts, skills, and abilities God has given us so that we may live the life we were created for!

DAY 4: VOICE OF TRUTH

Read chapter 10 of the *She Dreams* book, "Voice of Truth," noting below any insights or encouragement you gain from your reading:

Extra Insight

The Amalekites were descendants of Amalek, the grandson of Esau (see Genesis 36:12, 16). One source observes: "No doubt they regarded the Sinaitic region as their own, and as the most valuable portion of their territory, since it contained their summer and autumn pastures....They would regard the Israelites as intruders, robbers, persons entitled to scant favour at their hands."[2]

> [margin]
>
> ¹⁴Wise words bring many benefits,
>   and hard work brings rewards.
>
> ¹⁵Fools think their own way is right,
>   but the wise listen to others.
>
> ¹⁶A fool is quick-tempered,
>   but a wise person stays calm when insulted.
>
> ¹⁷An honest witness tells the truth;
>   a false witness tells lies.
>
> ¹⁸Some people make cutting remarks,
>   but the words of the wise bring healing.
>
> ¹⁹Truthful words stand the test of time,
>   but lies are soon exposed.
> (Proverbs 12:14-19)

Desribe in your own words the role of a wise encourager:

Today you read about a mentor of mine who has been a voice of truth in my life. He is a mentor who knows me, believes in what God is doing in my life, and is committed to leading me to closer to Christ. I hardly make any major life decision without first listening to his wise words. He has encouraged me on several occasions, and I wouldn't be who I am today without his kind voice of wisdom and truth.

Have you had someone in your life who has been an encouraging voice of truth? If so, describe the character and values of this person:

What words of wisdom have been particularly helpful as you pursue your dreams?

Often the godly men and women who are up close and personal—those familiar with the details of our lives—are able to offer us words of wisdom and truth. They know our strengths, our weaknesses, and our dreams. Their words of encouragement and advice can serve us well as we pursue the dreams God has placed within our hearts.

According to Proverbs 12:14-19 (in margin), it is important to listen to wisdom and truth because they keep us calm, bring healing, and help us to recognize what is true. Someone who passionately loves God and is farther along on the journey of life will be able to give us what we cannot give ourselves: wisdom we need for our own journey in order to reach our dreams. If you are in a season when you don't feel you have someone with whom you can share your struggles, research someone who is doing what you long to do or accomplish, or ask friends who might know of someone who could offer advice and wisdom. There is likely someone in your world or your friends' world who could give you timely and helpful encouragement for the road ahead!

On what subject would you benefit from hearing timely wisdom?

Who in your world is an expert on this subject, or who might know of someone who is an expert on this subject?

From parenting to house flipping to hand lettering, there is likely someone who can offer you wise advice as you pursue your dreams. He or she might not know the ins and outs of your situation but can encourage you to keep pursuing your dreams as you grow through your obstacles.

DAY 5: PERMISSION TO ASK FOR HELP

As we wrap up Week 5 of our study, I hope you are encouraged to pursue your dreams and live the life you were created for! As we've learned this week, pursuing our dreams provides ample opportunity for personal growth as we trust God with every inch of our dream. Growing pains are part of the journey, something we can't avoid; but when we refuse to compare ourselves with others, recognize the provision God offers, use what's in our hands, and listen to voices of truth, we are then able to move forward—one step at a time—and become women who can handle the God-sized dreams in our hearts!

Today we will take a closer look at the exchange between Jethro and Moses in Exodus 18. The last time Jethro and Moses were together was when Moses requested to leave Midian and return to Egypt (Exodus 4:18). It has been some time since then, and Jethro visits Moses in the wilderness.

Read Exodus 18 in your Bible. How does Jethro communicate care and affection for Moses?

Extra Insight

The Midianites were descendants of Abraham and, like the Israelites, worshiped the God of Abraham, Isaac, and Jacob. Though they were willing to worship God, they most likely did not know God as Jehovah. However, Jethro clearly understood that the God Moses served was sovereign and supreme over all the earth.[3]

Based on this passage, how would you describe the relationship between Moses and Jethro?

Why do you think Moses was willing to listen to the wise advice of Jethro?

How did Moses grow through this experience?

Jethro had Moses' best interests at heart. He wanted to witness Moses succeed at what God had called him to do. Moses was not only the great emancipator of the Old Testament but also Jethro's son-in-law. Moses knew the affection Jethro felt toward him and didn't dismiss Jethro's advice in favor of the way he had been conducting matters. He listened and heeded Jethro's advice, and everyone won when he did. If folks in the camp had complaints, they no longer had to wait for Moses to mediate the matter but instead approached their governing head. Let's not kid ourselves; Moses had enough to worry about. So this advice radically changed the order of his days when he shared the responsibility with other capable leaders.

Sometimes we feel that we have to do it all or it won't happen. We fear that if we share the burden or load, then things won't happen exactly the way we'd like; but that isn't necessarily true. As we listen to wise advice, we'll find that we don't have to do it all to see our dreams come to pass. We can do only what we can do. If there are others with willing hands and hearts in our lives who can help us reach our dreams, we can ask them for assistance, inviting them to play a role that we can't complete on our own. Sometimes it takes the advice of a wise sage to remind us that we can ask for help. We aren't invincible, and we can't do it all.

Earlier we identified that Moses had a helper—his brother, Aaron. Name other helpers Moses has had up to this point and the way in which each helped Moses pursue the dream of freedom for the Israelites:

Helper	How He/She Helped
Aaron	He was a mouthpiece for Moses when he addressed Pharaoh.

How beautiful that Moses' dream of freedom for Israel invited others to use their skills and abilities for the glory of the Lord! Like Moses, our dreams come to pass not when we try to do it all but when we invite others to play a crucial part in the journey. Every person possesses God-given gifts and strengths; and as we invite others into our dream, we see that, together, the dream comes to pass.

Have you ever felt that you alone had to "make it happen" in order to see your dreams come to pass? If so, describe that feeling briefly.

Life is not a one-person show. We share our lives—our ups and downs, victories and failures, hopes and dreams—with those we trust. As we invite others into the dream and plan (as Moses did after Jethro's encouragement), we are able to do what only we can do. As we dream, we have to remember that others may be able to accomplish tasks that require time or skills we just don't have. In those moments, let's remember to do what only we can do, because friend, we can't do it all!

> Perhaps you could invite a pastor, friend, community leader, activist, or Bible study teacher who is in your life to speak into your pursuit of your dreams. When you think about those dreams, think of men and women who have journeyed toward their own dreams and may have something to offer. Approach them, ask for an hour of their time, and ask questions. Share your predicaments, dilemmas, and struggles. Most of us won't have a mentor show up in our world without an introduction. Go for it, girl. Even if someone says no, keep asking. You'll never know unless you ask. As, the Lord leads you, may you discover those who could be the voice of truth you need.
>
> —*She Dreams*, pages 164-165

Offer a prayer of gratitude for the voices of truth in your life and those who are helping to carry the dream forward. If you want, write your prayer below.

GROUP SESSION GUIDE: WEEK 5

Growing Pains

As we pursue our dreams, our gifts come to light through our challenges. We'll no doubt face challenges as we chase dreams, but we can be sure that spiritual growth is hidden in those challenges.

Welcome/Prayer/Icebreaker (5–10 minutes)

Welcome to session 5 of *She Dreams*! This week we learned that growing pains are part of the journey of dream chasing. But when we refuse to compare ourselves with others, recognize the provision God offers, use what's in our hands, and listen to voices of truth, we are then able to move forward—one step at a time—and become women who can handle the God-sized dreams in our hearts! Take a moment to open with prayer, and then go around the circle and share something that has felt like a growing pain as you've begun to dream about what God might do in and through you.

Video (about 25 minutes)

Play the video segment for session 5, completing the following notes as you watch. Feel free to add notes about anything that resonates with you or that you want to be sure to remember.

—*Video Notes*—

Scriptures: *Exodus* 15:26; 16:23, 28–29a; 17:15; 18:23; *1 Corinthians* 10:4

Our gifts on the journey to our dreams are hidden in the _____.

God _____ us where we are.

Growing Pains

Our challenges can _____ us if we let them.

We need _____ to see the dream become reality.

Group Discussion (20–25 minutes for a 60-minute session; 30–35 minutes for a 90-minute session)

Video Discussion

- God has given you a beautiful tribe to walk the journey with you. Ask this question: Where do you need encouragement, support, or help as you pursue your dreams?

Personal Lessons Review and Discussion

Day 1

1. Who we are, what God is doing within us, and the person we are becoming is unique, one-of-a-kind, and incredibly special. Rather than compare our looks, accomplishments, platform, or possessions, we can accept our story and live in the fullness of God.
   - Do you struggle with comparing your life to others around you or online? (page 105) What does that struggle look like for you?

Day 2

1. After their triumphant crossing of the Red Sea, the Israelites were led into the wilderness. They now had life before the Red Sea and life after the Red Sea. As they passed between the walls of water, they experienced a birth of sorts. Like a newborn they cried and whined for the comforts of familiar territory, but it was no longer time for them to be in Egypt; their time, their birth, had come, and they could not go back. Everything would be different, and they, like a newborn, were completely dependent on their Caregiver.
   - Read Exodus 15:22-27. What and how did God provide for the Israelites? (page 108)
   - Read Exodus 16:10. What is the significance of this verse? (page 109)

2. We often despise wilderness seasons, but God goes before us, leading the way for our good. God called the Israelites into the wilderness for their good, not their destruction. In the wilderness, God could prove Himself faithful without any distractions. He could become their Provider when they had no one else to rely on.
   - Have you ever experienced a wilderness season? How did God provide for your needs during that time?

Day 3

1. As we dream, we can use what's in our hand to move forward in our journey to see our dreams come to pass. Authors tap away on their keyboard, singers clutch a microphone, and painters wield their brush to create the masterpieces only they can create. We can't sit by and hope everything happens on its own; we must engage our skills and abilities as we trust the Lord.
   - What is in your "hand" that you can use as you partner with God for your dreams? (page 110)

2. In our low moments, the ones when we feel tormented, we can call out to God, listen to His instructions, and partner with Him to grow through our troubles. Complaining and arguing will never lead us to a place of greater trust and partnership with God.
   - Read Philippians 4:6. What does this verse tell us to do in our struggles? (page 112)
   - Review Exodus 17. What did the Israelites do instead of trusting God? Have you ever caught yourself complaining and arguing instead of taking the matter to the Lord in prayer? (page 112)

Day 4

1. Often, the godly men and women who are up close and personal—those familiar with the details of our lives—are able to offer us words of wisdom and truth. They know our strengths, our weaknesses, and our dreams. Their words of encouragement and advice can serve us well as we pursue the dreams God has placed within our hearts.
   - Who has been an encouraging voice of truth in your life? What wisdom that they've shared with you has been particularly helpful as you pursue your dreams? (page 114)

- Read Proverbs 12:14-19. What does this passage tell us about the power of voices of truth in our lives? (page 114)

Day 5
1. How beautiful that Moses' dream of freedom for Israel invited others to use their skills and abilities for the glory of the Lord! Like Moses, our dreams come to pass not when we try to do it all but when we invite others to play a crucial part in the journey. Every person possesses God-given gifts and strengths; and as we invite others into our dream, we see that, together, the dream comes to pass.
    - Review Exodus 18 and your notes from Day 5. How would you describe the relationship between Jethro and Moses? (page 117)
    - Who were Moses' helpers in pursuing his God-sized dream? (page 117) Who are some of the helpers in your journey, bringing their gifts and skills to help you live into your dream?

2. Life is not a one-person show. We share our lives—our ups and downs, victories and failures, hopes and dreams—with those we trust. As we invite others into the dream and plan (as Moses did after Jethro's encouragement), we are able to do what only we can do.
    - Have you ever felt that you alone had to "make it happen" in order to see your dreams come to pass? (page 117)
    - What did you learn about yourself through that experience? What did you learn about God?

Becoming a Dreamer (10–15 minutes—90-minute session only)

Divide into groups of two to three for the following:

- Spend some time digging into the ways in which comparison can cause your dreams to stall. Create some action steps that you can use when you feel comparison taking your eyes off of your dream.

Closing Prayer (5 minutes)

Close the session by sharing personal prayer requests and praying together. In addition to praying out loud for one another, ask God to bring to mind friends and helpers who will speak truth, encourage, and cheer you on in your dreams.

Week 6

Be(coming) the Dreamer

Moses Inspires Others to Dream
(Exodus 19:6–40)

*Your dreams shape your journey and
the journey of those around you.*

DAY 1: REFRESH YOURSELF

In this last week of our study, we'll examine the character Moses developed and the actions he took that ensured he not only pursued his dreams but others pursued their dreams as well. Like the dreams of Moses, our dreams are bigger than us, outshine us, and even outlive us as we chase the Dream Giver. Who we become in the process of pursuing our dreams—a woman of resolve, truth, and grace—is as precious as the dream itself and even invites other dreamers to rise up and chase after the Dream Giver!

Read chapter 11 of the *She Dreams* book, "Refresh Yourself," noting below any insights or encouragement you gain from your reading:

How would you describe the pace of your life? How do you spend your days?

We all have different ways we spend our days. Some of us have a slower pace, some have a quicker pace, and some have a combination of both. Certain seasons demand more of us; there are emotional, mental, and physical demands that can't be ignored or things just won't get done. However, we can't live with that pace forever. We were never intended to. A healthy pace requires self-awareness, honest reflection, and a willingness to adapt and change.

You read in chapter 11 how I once kept an impossible pace, one so busy that I could hardly tell myself what gave me joy. When we have multiple irons in the fire, it can seem like a waste of time to stop and examine what is working and what is not. Yet if we don't examine our lives in every season, we ignore the cries of our heart—cries that beg for change and cries that beg for rest.

Has there been a time in your life when you didn't feel like you had the privilege of rest? If so, describe it briefly:

So many of us feel that in order to succeed and reach our dreams, we must go harder, faster, stronger, and quicker than everyone else; but the way of the Dream Giver is better, slower, and sweeter. He is our Leader and Shepherd, and His ways invite peace, rest, and trust in His pace. Close your time today by meditating on Psalm 23:1-6 below, reflecting on the pace of life implied by the psalmist's words.

> ¹*The* Lord *is my shepherd;*
>   *I have all that I need.*
> ²*He lets me rest in green meadows;*
>   *he leads me beside peaceful streams.*
> ³*He renews my strength.*
> *He guides me along right paths,*
>   *bringing honor to his name.*
> ⁴*Even when I walk*
>   *through the darkest valley,*
> *I will not be afraid,*
>   *you are close beside me.*
> *Your rod and your staff*
>   *protect and comfort me.*
> ⁵*You prepare a feast for me*
>   *in the presence of my enemies.*
> *You honor me by anointing my head with oil.*
>   *My cup overflows with blessings.*

⁶Surely your goodness and unfailing love will pursue me
    all the days of my life,
and I will live in the house of the LORD
    forever.

DAY 2: THE REST GOD GIVES

Have you ever had those days when you come home and immediately get into comfy clothes, grab a cup of tea, and plop yourself on the couch with zero intention to move? I sure have! There are times when I think I can accomplish so much without feeling it. Then, of course, I crash on the couch with a heating pad on my back because I pushed myself farther than I should have. My body and mind cry out for rest, and you know what? Rest is a good thing. Rest is not sloth. Rest is a choice to unplug from all that we do and simply allow ourselves to be.

Describe a time when you desperately needed rest but didn't feel that you had a chance to rest:

God is a giver of rest. He knows all our needs, and He instituted the act of rest when He gave instructions for the Sabbath to the Israelites. Not only did He give instructions to the Israelites; He modeled rest. He knew Moses and the Israelites needed rest in order to reconnect with Him, recognize why they were pursuing freedom, and realign their priorities to honor Him.

Read Exodus 20:8-11 in the margin. According to these verses, why did God give instructions for the Sabbath?

Read Exodus 24:9-18 in your Bible. What happened on Mount Sinai?

⁸"Remember to observe the Sabbath day by keeping it holy. ⁹You have six days each week for your ordinary work, ¹⁰but the seventh day is a Sabbath day of rest dedicated to the LORD your God. On that day no one in your household may do any work. This includes you, your sons and daughters, your male and female servants, your livestock, and any foreigners living among you. ¹¹For in six days the LORD made the heavens, the earth, the sea, and everything in them; but on the seventh day he rested. That is why the LORD blessed the Sabbath day and set it apart as holy."

(Exodus 20:8-11)

Be(coming) the Dreamer

¹²One day Moses said to the LORD, "You have been telling me, 'Take these people up to the Promised Land.' But you haven't told me whom you will send with me. You have told me, 'I know you by name, and I look favorably on you.' ¹³If it is true that you look favorably on me, let me know your ways so I may understand you more fully and continue to enjoy your favor. And remember that this nation is your very own people."

¹⁴The LORD replied, "I will personally go with you, Moses, and I will give you rest—everything will be fine for you."

(Exodus 33:12-14)

What was different on the seventh day?

Now read Exodus 33:12-14 in the margin. Why do you think Moses asked the Lord who would go with him?

What did God promise Moses?

While chapters 20–23 of Exodus record parts of the Law given to Moses by God on Mount Sinai, it's worth noting how they were given to Moses. Moses ceased from his daily responsibilities and sat in the presence of God atop the mountain. He was given time to reconnect with God, which I can imagine was much needed considering how much complaining and criticizing from the Israelites he had handled. He was able to recognize once again why they were pursuing freedom: to become a holy nation, a kingdom of priests that would be a blessing to the rest of the world. He was given instructions to realign their way of living (the Law) with God to honor Him with their bodies and actions. All of this happened when he stopped, unplugged, and allowed the Dream Giver to lead.

Throughout Exodus we see that the Israelites craved rest. They craved rest from their oppressors. They craved rest from toil. They craved rest for their families. They desired what you and I desire today: the basics. They had nothing of permanence, only the hope of rest. The kind of rest they desperately wanted—political, physical, emotional, and spiritual—would take them months, years, and even decades to find. Sometimes it takes us that long too. Sometimes we ache and groan for rest but choose to run ourselves ragged, overcome by fear and doubt, when our souls scream for rest.

> God called Moses to lead His people to freedom so they could enter into rest. It was part of His restorative plan to His beloved people. In our modern way of doing things, many of us feel the never-ending weight of transition and fear that

> the Israelites likely felt. We think we must prove ourselves, or we find ourselves in a season where we feel trapped by circumstances we can't control. No matter how the hustle finds us, rest is a holy practice that honors the Lord and makes room for our souls to breathe.
>
> —*She Dreams*, page 179

To rest is to resist controlling every detail of every minute of our lives and trust God with our present and future. In rest we make room to reflect and re-create—to cease from the hustle and bustle and allow ourselves to be defined not by what we do but simply by who we are, a child of God. If God commanded the Israelites, who camped in the wilderness for forty years, to rest, then we can follow their lead and rest as well. Rest isn't only for those who are overworked; it's for all of us.

In your own words, define *rest*:

In rest, we reconnect with God, our Dream Giver. How do you reconnect with God? What practices silence the world around you so that you can spend time in the presence of God?

In rest, we recognize *why* we do what we do. Take time to reflect on why you are pursuing your dreams in the ways that you are. Ask yourself what is working and what is not. Record your thoughts below:

In rest, we realign our priorities and actions in order to pursue the dreams God has for us. Take a few moments to ponder what adjustments you need to make in your priorities and actions in

Be(coming) the Dreamer

order to pursue the dreams God has placed within you. Record your thoughts below:

In what ways do you think rest in God correlates with trust in God?

In rest, we make the big decisions that alter our life's trajectory, and in rest we grow to trust the Lord with those decisions. Fear, worry, and anxiety weigh heavy on our hearts, but in rest our souls are energized as they find respite in God.

When I'm overcome by worry, I sing one of my favorite worship songs that encourages me to trust God with my whole being. The lyrics remind me that God did not create me to worry or fear:

> But you created me to worship—daily,
> So I'ma leave it all right here.[1]

For forty years the Israelites wandered in the wilderness of the Sinai Peninsula. They were on a journey to find political, emotional, spiritual, and physical rest. Yet when faced with famine or warfare, they blamed and criticized Moses instead of seizing the opportunity to trust God for their protection and rest. Like the Israelites, we long for rest. Rest from a stressful job, complicated relationships, or constant transition is what we crave. We won't find rest in complaining or criticizing others; it will come when we trust God to refresh us and give us the rest we need.

When we deny ourselves rest in God, we spin our wheels trying to give ourselves what only God can give: assurance that comes by way of His presence. In rest, we can trust God for the victory, we can depend on Him to energize our hearts, and we can worship Him as we reflect on all He has done for us. Hallelujah!

Offer your trust to God in prayer as you rest in Him. If you want, write your prayer below.

DAY 3: DESTINY

Read chapter 12 of the *She Dreams* book, "Destiny," noting below any insights or encouragement you gain from your reading:

Today you read about the destiny of women who dreamed. Different women—all with the audacity and tenacity to pursue their dreams—changed their lives and changed their world around them. Those women, like you and me, are built with passions and gifts on purpose for a great purpose. As we've established throughout our study, great purposes and dreams come in all shapes, sizes, and colors. Never assume the dream God has placed within you will be glamorous and bring you riches and fame. The Lord never promised us ease, comfort, or glamour—even if the stories of our childhood often end with a princess, a crown, a kingdom to rule over, and a man to hold her close. In reality, God promised us Himself. Period. As we partner with our great Companion, we can chase after dreams that invite us to be the strongest, fiercest, and wisest versions of ourselves.

From the stories in chapter 12 of women who pursued their dreams, which ones inspire you the most? Why?

Similar to these women, how do your God-given gifts, skills, and grit work together as you pursue your dreams?

Just as you did at the end of Week 1 (page 30), write down all that you dream of, this time adding more details:

How has the scope or understanding of your dreams changed?

How will your life change if your dreams come to pass?

How will the lives of those around you change if your dreams come to pass?

Others will be encouraged and inspired as we chase our God-sized dreams if they see all that God is doing in and through us. Just as we bless others with our dreams, so we will be encouraged and inspired when we identify how the dreams of others richly bless us. As we become who God has destined us to be, the people in our world are immeasurably blessed.

Our man Moses pursued the dreams God placed deep within his heart, and others were immeasurably blessed as they identified what God had for them while those dreams came to pass. As he pursued freedom for the Israelites, Moses was given instructions for the temple of God, where the presence of God would reside with the Israelites at all times. At this point, God spoke directly to Moses, but He had plans to inhabit the place of His beloved people. In Exodus 35 God instructed them to build a tabernacle (God's Tent of Meeting) where the ark of the covenant (a golden rectangular box that contained the Ten Commandments and symbolized God's covenant with Israel) would reside in the Holy of Holies. How majestic!

Sadly, just a few chapters earlier in Exodus 32, the Israelites had erected a golden calf to worship in Moses' absence. Even though God's destiny for Israel was to lead them to a land flowing with milk and honey that they could call their own, they chose instead to melt down their gold and mold it into a calf! They praised the calf as if it were the one that had delivered them from Egypt. Moses was leading the Israelites to freedom by the goodness of God, but they didn't grasp all that God was doing through him for their benefit. The honest truth is that our destiny is beautiful and good and whole, yet we sabotage it when we take our eyes off the Dream Giver and fail to see how the dreams of others bless us.

We must remember that the Dream Giver will be with us every step of the way as we chase after the dreams of our hearts. As we see others pursuing their dreams, may it draw us closer to the Father, not farther away. It is never worth it to sacrifice the dreams of God for our own comfort, thinking that we know better. Never ever. What God has for us is always better!

Who has blessed you because she chased her dreams? Write her name below, and call or text this woman whose pursuit of her dreams has been a blessing to you.

DAY 4: INVITING OTHERS TO DREAM

Recently while listening to a podcast dedicated to encouraging women to pursue their passions, I heard the story of a start-up out of Dallas that produces fine leather goods. The dreamer, whose eye for fashion led her to spend her weeknights designing and sourcing leather for shoes, handbags, and accessories, worked as an administrative assistant by day. She spent weekends at trade shows alongside her husband/business partner sharing about their company, their mission, and their heart. Toward the end of her interview, she pleaded with women to pursue their dreams, surround themselves with others who believe in what God is doing within them, and get after it, even when it feels impossible. She unashamedly and unapologetically invited others to dream.

More often than not, we are paralyzed by fear, anxiety, or worry and forfeit the chase because we don't see how things could possibly bend our way. Even worse, after we've tried our best, things turn sour and we can't seem to keep the dream alive because the pressures of reality are too much to take. Then someone comes along—maybe it's someone who knows us well or someone who is being interviewed on a podcast—and she invites us to dream and keep on dreaming despite how grim things may be. Even with the odds stacked against us, we are told that we'll regret sitting it out when we were born to live the extraordinary life of a dreamer.

As we pursue our dreams—whether it be finishing a degree in counseling, launching a fine leather goods company, founding a nonprofit, or whatever it may be—we have the opportunity to invite others to chase the dreams that beat in their hearts! With our encouragement, which may hold more weight than we even realize, we can invite others to take their place as a dreamer too.

Have you ever been in the midst of fear and failure and had someone encourage you to pursue your dreams despite the disruptions and struggles? If so, describe the experience briefly:

Who in your world can you encourage to pursue her dreams even though she may be up against some tough obstacles?

Moses dealt with his fair share of complaining from the very people he was leading to freedom, which is to be expected when you are camped in a parched desert; but two men, Joshua and Caleb, were as confident as Moses was to follow after God and take the Promised Land God intended to give them.

Read the account of Joshua and Caleb and the other ten spies in Numbers 13, Numbers 14:1-9, and Numbers 14:26-33. Then answer the following questions:

How did Joshua and Caleb encourage the Israelites to trust God for their future?

Why do you think the Israelites chose fear rather than trusting God to deliver the Promised Land to them?

Be(coming) the Dreamer

Why do you think Joshua and Caleb were full of faith when others were frozen with fear?

What did the Israelites forfeit because of their fear?

The Israelites camped at Kadesh, which history tells us was only a few miles away from the Promised Land. They had been in the desert just two years before Moses sent the spies into the Promised Land to survey the land and its inhabitants. The terrifying report from ten of the spies led to widespread fear among the camp. This fear kept them from moving forward, and God would have none of it. For a total of forty years, an entire generation would miss out on the freedom they craved because they feared what God planned to conquer for them. Yet Joshua and Caleb took up Moses' invitation to trust God and dream bigger dreams rather than return to Egypt or stay in the wilderness out of fear. These two courageous men made their appeal to the masses to take the land that was promised to them. Although they were unsuccessful in convincing the leaders of Israel to seize the land God had promised to give them, their willingness to dream impossible dreams in the midst of impending struggles would be rewarded.

What were Joshua and Caleb promised in Numbers 14, and why?

We may face obstacles of all kinds, but as we become the dreamers God intends us to be, we are able to invite others to defy the odds and pursue the dreams that beat in their own hearts. God made us for His pleasure, to partner with Him in His purposes and invite others into the story God has for them. Just as Joshua and Caleb followed Moses' lead in trusting God's power and plan, we can remember the dreamers who have gone before us, allowing their stories of faithfulness to fuel our own fire to pursue our dreams and to invite other dreamers to chase after what God has placed in their hearts.

DAY 5: YOUR DREAMS WILL OUTSHINE YOU

This week we've seen Moses become the dreamer God created him to be through his actions, prayers, and ruthless trust in the Dream Giver. God invited Moses to rest in Him, promising Moses rest as he continued to lead the Israelites to the Promised Land (Exodus 33:14). Moses developed a deep trust in God while the Israelites questioned him and even erected a golden calf to worship instead of their Deliverer. The dreams God gave Moses must have felt impossible, and at times Moses was reluctant and fearful to pursue them; but still he continued moving toward the destiny God had for him, even inviting others to trust in the Dream Giver.

In our own lives, dreams can seem out of reach, tricky to chase after; and discouragement can knock on the door to our hearts. But who we become in the process is as important as, if not more important than, the dream itself. Remember, the God of heaven is after you. Communion with you is the dream of His heart. As you and I choose the way of the Father—not the easy way but the unique way mapped out for us—we become women of great resolve, strength, wisdom, and faith.

What kind of person do you desire to become as you pursue your dreams? Describe her below:

Today we'll examine how the dream of freedom for the people of God lived on long after Moses was gone. The dream God placed within him outshined him. I wonder if Moses had any idea just how impactful his role in human history would be. Do you think he knew that he would be one of the greatest prophets of the Old Testament? Do you think he knew his story would be told for thousands of years? I can't imagine he did.

A hard part of Moses' story is that he never entered into the Promised Land. He didn't enjoy the land flowing with milk and honey; but the Israelites, under

Extra Insight

The Israelites' forty years in the wilderness is detailed in Exodus, Leviticus, Numbers, and Deuteronomy.

Joshua's leadership, did. Can you believe it? After he faced Pharaoh and camped for forty years in the wilderness, the dreamer didn't get to enjoy the dream—at least not in person. Yet as we read in the following passages, the dream lived on even after he was gone:

> ⁴⁸That same day the LORD said to Moses, ⁴⁹"Go to Moab, to the mountains east of the river, and climb Mount Nebo, which is across from Jericho. Look out across the land of Canaan, the land I am giving to the people of Israel as their own special possession. ⁵⁰Then you will die there on the mountain. You will join your ancestors, just as Aaron, your brother, died on Mount Hor and joined his ancestors. ⁵¹For both of you betrayed me with the Israelites at the waters of Meribah at Kadesh in the wilderness of Zin. You failed to demonstrate my holiness to the people of Israel there. ⁵²So you will see the land from a distance, but you may not enter the land I am giving to the people of Israel."
>
> (Deuteronomy 32:48-52)

> ¹Then Moses went up to Mount Nebo from the plains of Moab and climbed Pisgah Peak, which is across from Jericho. And the LORD showed him the whole land, from Gilead as far as Dan; ²all the land of Naphtali; the land of Ephraim and Manasseh; all the land of Judah, extending to the Mediterranean Sea; ³the Negev; the Jordan Valley with Jericho—the city of palms—as far as Zoar. ⁴Then the LORD said to Moses, "This is the land I promised on oath to Abraham, Isaac, and Jacob when I said, 'I will give it to your descendants.' I have now allowed you to see it with your own eyes, but you will not enter the land."
>
> ⁵So Moses, the servant of the LORD, died there in the land of Moab, just as the LORD had said. ⁶The LORD buried him in a valley near Beth-peor in Moab, but to this day no one knows the exact place. ⁷Moses was 120 years old when he died, yet his eyesight was clear, and he was as strong as ever. ⁸The people of Israel mourned for Moses on the plains of Moab for thirty days, until the customary period of mourning was over.
>
> ⁹Now Joshua son of Nun was full of the spirit of wisdom, for Moses had laid his hands on him. So the people of Israel obeyed him, doing just as the LORD had commanded Moses.
>
> ¹⁰There has never been another prophet in Israel like Moses, whom the LORD knew face to face. ¹¹The LORD sent him to perform all the miraculous signs and wonders in the land of Egypt against Pharaoh, and all his servants, and his entire land. ¹²With mighty power, Moses performed terrifying acts in the sight of all Israel.
>
> (Deuteronomy 34:1-12)

> ¹After the death of Moses the LORD's servant, the LORD spoke to Joshua son of Nun, Moses' assistant. He said, ²"Moses my servant is dead. Therefore, the time has come for you to lead these people, the Israelites, across the Jordan River into the land I

am giving them. ³I promise you what I promised Moses: 'Wherever you set foot, you will be on land I have given you— ⁴from the Negev wilderness in the south to the Lebanon mountains in the north, from the Euphrates River in the east to the Mediterranean Sea in the west, including all the land of the Hittites.' ⁵No one will be able to stand against you as long as you live. For I will be with you as I was with Moses. I will not fail you or abandon you.

(Joshua 1:1-5)

⁴³So the Lord gave to Israel all the land he had sworn to give their ancestors, and they took possession of it and settled there. ⁴⁴And the Lord gave them rest on every side, just as he had solemnly promised their ancestors. None of their enemies could stand against them, for the Lord helped them conquer all their enemies. ⁴⁵Not a single one of all the good promises the Lord had given to the family of Israel was left unfulfilled; everything he had spoken came true.

(Joshua 21:43-45)

In your own words, describe how the dream of freedom for Israel outshined Moses:

The life of Moses was not defined by his failure to enter into the Promised Land. In fact, he is mentioned several times in the New Testament as a great prophet and deliverer of Israel. In addition to his honorable mentions by other biblical characters, "Moses foreshadows Jesus Christ in his role as a law-giver, as a mediator between God and his people and as a prophet who declared the will of God."² What started in Moses, Jesus brought to perfect completion.

Look up the following sets of verses, and briefly describe for each the parallels made between Moses and Jesus:

Exodus 1:22; 2:2
Matthew 2:12, 16

Be(coming) the Dreamer

Exodus 2:11, 15, 22
Deuteronomy 34:4
Matthew 2:13; 8:20

Exodus 4:5-9
Matthew 3:17

Exodus 19:3-9
Hebrews 9:15

Exodus 33:11
John 5:20

Deuteronomy 34:10
John 6:14
Acts 3:22

Exodus 34:33-35
2 Corinthians 3:18

Numbers 12:7
Hebrews 3:1-6

Not only did Moses lead the Israelites out of Egypt; his life foreshadowed our ultimate Deliverer, Jesus Christ—our prophet, priest, and King. Long after

Moses was gone, the dream of freedom for the Israelites led to the freedom in Christ that you and I enjoy today! Praise God!

Like Moses, when we partner with God for the dreams He has for us, we live a life that will far exceed our expectations. We may face disasters, wander, wait, and see our dreams come to pass, but even then we may not fully understand the impact our dreams will have. More often than not, our dreams will outshine us and others will be blessed beyond measure in ways we never could have dreamed of!

> You may feel like you don't have much to offer in your current season of life, but I dare you to look around and identify the folks in your world whose dreams might come to pass if you were to share your skills, gifts, talents, connections, compassion, wisdom, and resources. Who might they become as they chase the dreams in their hearts because of your investment and generosity?
>
> —*She Dreams*, page 195

As we wrap up our study on Moses, I pray that you've been challenged and encouraged and that you sense the urgency and importance of pursuing your dreams. Your dreams matter. Your passions, skills, and gifts all play a part as you chase after the wild dreams that burn in your heart. It doesn't matter where you came from or whether you were born with much or little. It doesn't matter the education you have, the failures you've experienced, the pharaohs in your life, or the road ahead, because your Dream Giver goes before you, leading you every step. Don't wait. Listen to the whisper, chase the dream, and live the life you were created for!

Write a final statement declaring your trust in the Dream Giver and your commitment to the dream:

GROUP SESSION GUIDE: WEEK 6

Becoming the Dreamer

*God gives us our dreams and
then God fulfills our dreams.*

Welcome/Prayer/Icebreaker (5–10 minutes)

Welcome to session 6 of *She Dreams*. In the final week of our study, we examined the character Moses developed and the actions he took that ensured not only that he pursued his dreams but others pursued their dreams as well. Take a moment to open with prayer, and then go around the circle and share someone else's dream that has been an inspiration to you as you chase after your own dream.

Video (about 25 minutes)

Play the video segment for session 6, completing the following notes as you watch. Feel free to add notes about anything that resonates with you or that you want to be sure to remember.

—Video Notes—

Scriptures: Exodus 19; Numbers 13; Deuteronomy 18:18; 34:8-12; Joshua 1:1-3; 3:7; 5:13-15; 21:43-45

God not only gives dreams; He _____ them.

The road to your dreams can be a _____ one.

Others experience the Dream Giver because of our _____ to the dream.

We may never know the full extent of how our dreams _____ _____.

Group Discussion (20–25 minutes for a 60-minute session; 30–35 minutes for a 90-minute session)

Video Discussion

- How might your God-given dream inspire and benefit others? Share your thoughts with the women in your group, and give yourselves permission to dream big about the potential impact of your dreams

Personal Lessons Review and Discussion

Day 1

1. We all have different ways we spend our days. Some of us have a slower pace, some have a quicker pace, and some have a combination of both. A healthy pace requires self-awareness, honest reflection, and a willingness to adapt and change.
   - How would you describe the pace of your life? How do you spend your days? (page 125)

2. So many of us feel that in order to succeed and reach our dreams, we must go harder, faster, stronger, and quicker than everyone else; but the way of the Dream Giver is better, slower, and sweeter.
   - Take turns reading Psalm 23. What is the pace of life implied by the psalmist?
   - What is required to get from your current pace to the pace of the psalmist?

Day 2

1. God is a giver of rest. He knows all our needs, and He instituted the act of rest when He gave instructions for the Sabbath to the Israelites. Not only did He give instructions to the Israelites, He modeled rest.
   - Describe a time when you desperately needed rest, but didn't feel that you had a chance to rest. (page 127)
   - Read Exodus 20:8-11. Why did God give instructions for the Sabbath? (page 127)

2. Throughout Exodus we see that the Israelites *craved* rest. They craved rest from their oppressors. They craved rest from toil. They craved rest for their families. They desired what you and I desire today: the basics.
   - Share your definition of rest on page 129.
   - In rest we reconnect with God, our Dream Giver. How do you reconnect with God? What practices silence the world around you so that you can spend time in the presence of God?

Day 3

1. As we partner with our great Companion, we can chase after dreams that invite us to be the strongest, fiercest, and wisest versions of ourselves.
   - Refer to your notes about chapter 12 on page 132. Which stories of women pursuing their dreams inspired you most? Why?

Day 4

1. As we pursue our dreams—whether it be finishing a degree in counseling, launching a fine leather goods company, founding a nonprofit, or whatever it may be—we have the opportunity to invite others to chase the dreams that beat in their hearts! With our encouragement, which may hold more weight than we even realize, we can invite others to take their place as dreamers too.
   - When have you been in the midst of fear and failure and had someone encourage you to pursue your dreams despite the disruptions and struggles? (page 135)

2. We may face obstacles of all kinds, but as we become the dreamers God intends us to be, we are able to invite others to pursue the dreams that beat in their own hearts. God made us for His pleasure, to partner with His purposes and invite others into the story God has for them.
   - Take turns reading Numbers 14. What were Joshua and Caleb promised? Why? (page 136)

Day 5

1. Dreams can seem out of reach, tricky to chase after, and discouragement can knock on the door to our hearts. Remember the God of heaven is after you. But who we become in the process is as important as the dream itself. Communion with you is the dream of God's heart. As we choose the way of the Father, we become women of great resolve, strength, wisdom, and faith.

- What kind of person do you desire to become as you pursue your dreams? (page 137)

2. A hard part of Moses' story is that he never entered into the Promised Land. He didn't enjoy the land flowing with milk and honey; but the Israelites, under Joshua's leadership, did. After he faced Pharaoh and camped for forty years in the wilderness, the dreamer didn't get to enjoy the dream—at least not in person. But the dream lived on even after he was gone.
   - Review Joshua 1:1-5 and 21:43-45. How did the dream of freedom for Israel outshine Moses? (page 139)
   - What do you hope the lasting legacy of your dream might be?

Becoming a Dreamer (10–15 minutes—90-minute session only)

Divide into groups of two to three for the following:

- Review your notes from Day 3 on page 132 about the full scope of your dream, with all the details. How has the scope or understanding of your dreams changed? How will your life change if your dreams come to pass? How will the lives of those around you change if your dreams come to pass?

Closing Prayer (5 minutes)

Close the session by sharing personal prayer requests and praying together. In addition to praying out loud for one another, give thanks to God for your time together in this study. Ask God to give you boldness, perseverance, and helpers along the way as you chase after your God-sized dreams!

Leader Helps

Tips for Facilitating a Group

Important Information

Before the first session you will want to distribute copies of the *She Dreams* book and this study guide to the members of your group. Be sure to communicate that they are to complete the first week in the study guide before your first group session. For each week there are five days of readings or lessons. On two days they will read a chapter in the *She Dreams* book, along with a short reading in the study guide; and on three days the lessons will guide them through Scripture study and reflection.

As you gather each week with the members of your group, you will have the opportunity to watch a video, discuss and respond to what you're learning, and pray together. You will need access to a television and DVD player with working remotes. Use the Group Session Guide at the end of each week's lesson to facilitate the session (options are provided for both a 60-minute and 90-minute format). In addition to these guides, the Group Session Guide Leader Notes (pages 149–154) provide additional helps including a Main Objective, Bible Overview, and Key Scriptures for each session.

Creating a warm and inviting atmosphere will help to make the women feel welcome. Although optional, you might consider providing snacks for your first meeting and inviting group members to rotate in bringing refreshments each week.

As group leader, your role is to guide and encourage the women on the journey to discover their God-sized dreams. Ensure that group members do not give unsolicited advice or opinions and that each person has the freedom to dream big. Pray for your group before the meetings, that God would pour out His Spirit on your time together, that the Spirit would stir up holy dreams and passions, and that in your six-week community you will gain encouragement, confidence, and strength to pursue the dreams God has put in your hearts.

Preparing for the Sessions

- Be sure to communicate dates and times to participants in advance.
- Be sure that group members have their books and study guides at least one week before your first session and instruct them to complete the first week of personal lessons in the study guide. (As they complete the lessons, they will be instructed to read two chapters of the book during the week, as well.) If you have the phone numbers or e-mail addresses of your group members, send out a reminder and a welcome.

- Check out your meeting space before each group session. Make sure the room is ready. Do you have enough chairs? Do you have the equipment and supplies you need? (See the list of materials that follows.)
- Pray for your group and each group member by name. Ask God to work in the life of every woman in your group.
- Read and complete the week's readings in this study guide as well as the corresponding book chapters, and review the group session guide. Select the discussion points and questions you want to cover and make some notes in the margins to share in your discussion time.

Leading the Sessions

- Personally welcome and greet each woman as she arrives. Take attendance if desired.
- To create a warm, welcoming environment as the women are gathering before the session begins, consider lighting one or more candles, providing coffee or other refreshments, and/or playing worship music. (Bring an iPod, smartphone, or tablet and a portable speaker if desired.) Be sure to provide name tags if the women do not know one another or you have new participants in your group.
- Always start on time. Honor the time of those who are on time.
- At the start of each session, ask the women to turn off or silence their cell phones.
- Communicate the importance of completing the weekly lessons and participating in group discussion.
- Encourage everyone to participate fully, but don't put anyone on the spot. Invite the women to share as they are comfortable. Be prepared to offer a personal example or answer if no one else responds at first.
- Facilitate but don't dominate. Remember that if you talk most of the time, group members may tend to listen rather than to engage. Your task is to encourage conversation and keep the discussion moving.
- If someone monopolizes the conversation, kindly thank her for sharing and ask if anyone else has any insights.
- Try not to interrupt, judge, or minimize anyone's comments or input.
- Remember that you are not expected to be the expert or have all the answers. Acknowledge that all of you are on this journey together, with the Holy Spirit as your leader and guide. If issues or questions

arise that you don't feel equipped to handle or answer, talk with the pastor or a staff member at your church.
- Don't rush to fill the silence. If no one speaks right away, it's okay to wait for someone to answer. After a moment, ask, "Would anyone be willing to share?" If no one responds, try asking the question again a different way—or offer a brief response and ask if anyone has anything to add.
- Encourage good discussion, but don't be timid about calling time on a particular question and moving ahead. Part of your responsibility is to keep the group on track. If you decide to spend extra time on a given question or activity, consider skipping or spending less time on another question or activity in order to stay on schedule.
- Try to end on time. If you are running over, give members the opportunity to leave if they need to. Then wrap up as quickly as you can.
- Thank the women for coming and let them know you're looking forward to seeing them next time.
- Be prepared for some women to want to hang out and talk at the end. If you need everyone to leave by a certain time, communicate this at the beginning of the group session. If you are meeting in a church during regularly scheduled activities, be aware of nursery closing times.

Materials Needed

- *She Dreams* book and study guide
- *She Dreams* DVD and a DVD player
- Stick-on name tags and markers (optional)
- iPod, smartphone, or tablet and portable speaker (if desired for gathering music)

Group Session Guide Leader Notes

Use these notes for your own review and preparation; and if desired, you can share them with the group at the beginning of the session (minus the Scriptures). The Main Objective and Bible Story Overview can help to set the tone for the session as well as prepare everyone for the group discussion, especially those who might have been unable to complete their personal lessons during the week.

Session 1: You Were Born for This

Main Objective
To give voice to our God-given dreams and begin to take steps toward pursuing them.

Main Scripture
Exodus 1:1–2:15

Bible Story Overview
Throughout our study we will be following the story of Moses, which is full of losses, gains, bravery, doubt, and victory. Moses grew in strength, faith, and tenacity for the ways of God, and one day God's dream for him became the dream of his own heart.

Even as a baby, Moses was fighting for his life as Pharaoh ordered the death of all Hebrew baby boys. Because of the bravery of some midwives, Moses survived. His mother, his sister, and his adoptive mother (Pharaoh's daughter) violated Pharaoh's order and made a way for Moses to live in the king's palace—with his own mother and sister to care for him! As he grew, Moses was cared for and educated with all the privileges of a son of the royal court. But with the knowledge that he was an outsider living a privileged Egyptian life, the grown-up Moses experienced a broken heart when he saw the suffering of the enslaved Israelites who were forced to work under such harsh conditions. His broken heart would be a catalyst for a God-sized dream.

Session 2: God-Sized Dreams

Main Objective
To recognize that our God-sized dreams will be bigger than anything we could ever do on our own.

Main Scripture
Exodus 2:15–4:17

Bible Story Overview
Moses was on the run after killing an Egyptian. The Hebrew slaves knew what he had done, and it didn't take long for Pharaoh to find out as well. Moses' life was in danger because he had committed a crime punishable by death, and so he escaped to Midian, a safe place to hide.

In Midian, Moses was a stranger in a foreign land—not the royalty he had been in Egypt. He was starting over with nothing as he wondered what his next steps would be. But even as an outlaw, Moses was still called by God for great and mighty purposes. He did not disown his passions in Midian but, even there, saw opportunities to defend and protect. His conviction and compassion led him to Reuel (or Jethro), who loved God and eventually loved Moses.

Later Moses encountered the One true God of Israel whose plans would become his wildest dreams. God appeared to Moses in a burning bush and called him to a great task. Moses had some disbelief that he would be the one to lead the Israelites to freedom, but God persisted, performing some miracles to convince Moses that God is who He says He is.

After some back and forth with God, Moses asked for God's name so that he could tell the Israelites who had sent him, to which God responded that His name is "I AM." God's very name would be an encouragement that God would be with Moses every step of the way. God also provided a way to let Moses' brother, Aaron, be his mouthpiece because Moses couldn't see past his lack of speaking skills. Even before Moses made his way back to Egypt, God had people in place to support Moses as he pursued the dreams God had placed in his heart.

Session 3: Fighting for the Dream

Main Objective
To discover that dreams require our constant participation even as we trust the Lord for victory.

Main Scripture
Exodus 4:18–12:32

Bible Story Overview
This week the plan starts to unfold a little more. With support and blessing from his father-in-law and confirmation from God, Moses met up with Aaron in the wilderness. The two of them returned to Egypt and called the elders of Israel together. Once in Egypt, Moses made his way to meet Pharaoh and requested to hold a festival in the wilderness. Pharaoh was not pleased to oblige. In fact, Pharaoh increased the workload of the Israelites, sending a message to Moses and Aaron saying that he held the power.

God, who was and is the real power at work, equipped Moses with a message both for the Israelites and for Pharaoh: let the Israelites go free. Moses had another conversation with God that resulted in just enough crazy courage to demand once again that Pharaoh let God's people go. God even gave Moses some signs to perform as a show of His strength.

Moses and Aaron worked together to demand freedom for God's people, but Pharaoh's hardened heart would not succumb to their demands or the series of plagues. Finally, Pharaoh gave in when the firstborn boys of Egypt died due to his own hardened heart and refusal to listen to God's warning. The stubborn king of Egypt let the Israelites go only to change his mind. Through it all, Moses' dream required constant participation and trust that God would bring a victory.

Session 4: Don't Give Up on the Daydream

Main Objective
To affirm that when the going gets tough, God is still in control. He is still the Dream Giver!

Main Scripture
Exodus 12:32–15:21

Bible Story Overview
This week we saw Pharaoh making his last-ditch effort to stop his free labor from making their grand exit. God led the Israelites to the Promised Land, knowing what they could handle and their ingrained reliance on the power and providence of Pharaoh. He led them to a place where their Egyptian oppressors would assume they could catch them, but what happened was a witness to the power of the Lord.

The Israelites journeyed on foot even as they saw their oppressors chasing them in chariots. They groaned to Moses, asking why he had brought them out of Egypt only to be pursued by Pharaoh and die. In a moment of what seemed like sure defeat, God instructed Moses to raise his staff; and the Red Sea parted, making a way for the Israelites to get to the other side. God in His sovereignty did the miraculous work of providing a way through the waters.

When the last Israelite stepped onto the bank, Moses let down his staff and the waters closed back in, washing away the Egyptian army. After witnessing the mighty power that the Lord had unleashed against the Egyptians, the people of Israel were filled with awe and put their faith in the Lord and in His servant Moses.

Session 5: Growing Pains

Main Objective
To discover that pursuing our dreams provides ample opportunites for spiritual growth.

Main Scripture
Exodus 15:22–19:6

Bible Story Overview

After their triumphant crossing of the Red Sea, the Israelites were led into the wilderness. God had a good plan that would test them and build them into the nation He desired them to be, but now they had to trust God for their every need instead of relying on their oppressors for food and housing. By their complaints we can gather that the Israelites were not raving fans of their new conditions. Yet God was present with them in the wilderness, available and willing to meet their needs. God called them into the wilderness for their good, not their destruction. There God could prove Himself faithful without any distractions; He could become their Provider when they had no one else to rely on.

Moses knew a thing or two about trusting the Lord, but the Israelites were not as spiritually mature. They complained to Moses, criticizing him for their lack of drinking water. They worried that God would not provide. But God, in His providence, partnered with Moses to supply clean drinking water by way of his staff.

Rather than cry out to God for water, the Israelites complained to Moses. Even though they had witnessed God's power and provision, they chose to argue and test rather than petition and pray.

Session 6: Be(coming) the Dreamer

Main Objective

To embrace the truth that our dreams shape not only our own journeys but also the journeys of those around us.

Main Scripture

Exodus 19:6–40

Bible Story Overview

As Moses pursued the dreams God had placed deep within his heart, others were immeasurably blessed as well, identifying what God had for them in the fulfillment of those dreams. As he pursued freedom for the Israelites, Moses received from God instructions for the Tabernacle, where His presence would reside with His people. Within this tabernacle, the ark of the covenant would be placed in the Holy of Holies.

Though Moses dealt with many complainers, two men, Joshua and Caleb, were confident in Moses' dream. These two courageous men took up Moses' invitation to trust God and dream bigger dreams, appealing to the masses to take the land that was promised to them. But fear and disobedience resulted in the Israelites spending forty years in the wilderness. Only the younger generation of Israelites, plus Joshua and Caleb, would eventually enter the land.

A hard part of Moses' story is that he never entered into the Promised Land. After Moses faced Pharaoh and camped for forty years in the wilderness, the dreamer didn't get to enjoy the dream. But the dream lived on even after he was gone as the mantle of leadership was passed to Joshua. Rather than his life being defined by his failure to enter into the Promised Land, Moses is remembered as a great leader and one who foreshadowed Christ's role as lawgiver, mediator between God and His people, and prophet who declared the will of God. Long after Moses was gone, the dream of freedom for the Israelites led to the freedom in Christ that is available to all today.

Notes

Week 1

1. Herbert Locyear, "Pharaoh's Daughter," in *All the Women of the Bible* (Grand Rapids, MI: Zondervan, 1988); see also Bible Gateway, https://www.biblegateway.com/resources/all-women-bible/Pharaoh-8217-s-Daughter, accessed July 10, 2018.

Week 2

1. David Guzik, "Enduring Word Bible Commentary Exodus Chapter 2." *Enduring Word*, https://enduringword.com/bible-commentary/exodus-2, accessed July 10, 2018.
2. "Prince Moses Escapes to Midian," *The Bible Journey*, www.thebiblejourney.org/biblejourney2/25-the-israelites-journey-from-egypt-to-mt-sinai/prince-moses-escapes-to-midian, accessed July 10, 2018.
3. *Ellicott's Commentary for English Readers*, s.v. "Exodus 2," http://biblehub.com/commentaries/ellicott/exodus/2.htm, accessed July 10, 2018.
4. *Matthew Henry's Commentary*, s.v. "Exodus 3," http://biblehub.com/commentaries/mhc/exodus/3.htm, accessed July 10, 2018.
5. *Gill's Exposition*, s.v., "Exodus 3," http://biblehub.com/commentaries/gill/exodus/3.htm, accessed July 10, 2018.
6. *MacLaren Expositions of Holy Scripture*, s.v. "Exodus 3," https://biblehub.com/commentaries/maclaren/exodus/3.htm, accessed July 10, 2018.
7. *Benson Commentary*, s.v. "Exodus 4," https://biblehub.com/commentaries/benson/exodus/4.htm, accessed July 10, 2018.
8. Ibid.

Week 3

1. Taylor Swift, "Shake It Off," track 6 on Taylor Swift, *1989*, Big Machine Records, 2014, https://www.taylorswift.com/releases#/release/12453.
2. Adam Hamilton, *Moses: In the Footsteps of the Reluctant Prophet* (Nashville: Abingdon Press, 2017), 90.
3. Hamilton, 86–87.
4. New Living Translation Second Edition Life Application Study Bible (Wheaton, IL: Tyndale House, 2004), 112.

Week 4

1. "Red Sea Crossing," *Ashbury Bible Commentary*, https://www.biblegateway.com/resources/asbury-bible-commentary/Red-Sea-Crossing, accessed July 10, 2018.
2. Ibid.

Week 5

1. "Exodus 17," Ellicott's Commentary for English Readers, http://biblehub.com/commentaries/ellicott/exodus/17.htm, accessed July 10, 2018.
2. Ibid.
3. "Exodus 18," Ellicott's Commentary for English Readers, http://biblehub.com/commentaries/ellicott/exodus/18.htm, accessed July 10, 2018.

Week 6

1. Anthony Brown & Group TherAPy, "Trust In You," track 10 on *Anthony Brown & Group TherAPy, A Long Way from Sunday*, Fair Trade/Columbia, 2017, www.metrolyrics.com/trust-in-you-lyrics-anthony-brown-group-therapy.html.
2. "5104 Moses, Foreshadower of Jesus Christ," https://www.biblegateway.com/resources/dictionary-of-bible-themes/5104-Moses-foreshadower-Jesus, accessed July 10, 2018.

Also from Tiffany Bluhm

In the *Never Alone* Bible study, Tiffany invites us to find healing for our hurts as we experience the unfailing companionship of Jesus. This six-week study reveals the healing power of Jesus' unconditional love through encounters He had with six hurting women in the Gospels: the woman caught in adultery, hemorrhaging woman, woman at the well, woman who anointed Him, Mary Magdalene, and Mary, Jesus' mother.

Never Alone: 6 Encounters with Jesus to Heal Your Deepest Hurts
Bible Study Components

Participant Workbook | 9781501845826
DVD | 9781501845864
Leader Guide | 978151845840
Leader Kit | 9781501845871

Never Alone: Exchanging Your Tender Hurts for God's Healing Grace
Book | 9781501848636

Praise for Never Alone: Exchanging Your Tender Hurts for God's Healing Grace

"Have you ever had your heart broken? Have you ever felt abandoned, unloved? If you have, you will find a friend in these pages. With disarming transparency, Tiffany walks us through her own heartbreak to the glorious realization of this truth: she has never been alone, and neither have we."

—**Sheila Walsh,** Author of *In The Middle of the Mess*

Find Samples at AbingdonWomen.com
Available Wherever Books are Sold.

Abingdon *Women*